Power Up Your Life
The GOGI Way:
The PowerUp! Manual

By Coach Taylor, GOGI Founder

This is another GOGI Book

Getting Out by Going In
P.O. Box 88969
Los Angeles, CA, USA 90009
www.gettingoutbygoingin.org

Power Up Your Life
The GOGI Way

Getting Out by Going In (GOGI) has a mission. Our mission is to empower communities with tools needed to build an extraordinary life.

Getting Out by Going In (GOGI) publishes its own materials and has a purpose for this book. This book is intended to provide all the information the reader will need to effectively learn, teach, inspire and support studies of the GOGI Tools.

GOGI currently offers these GOGI Tool study formats:

    1) Power Up! Community Meetings

    2) GOGI Self Study Courses and Group Certificate Program

    3) GOGI Learning Media

    4) GOGI Social Media Support

    5) GOGI Certified Community Coach Program

Getting Out by Going In (GOGI) is a non-profit organization. We develop and distribute educational materials sharing the simple GOGI Tools. We rely greatly on donations and volunteers to reach all populations. Getting Out by Going In (GOGI) offers self study courses at a discount. Donations fund these educational discounts so more individuals may learn the GOGI Tools.

ISBN: 978-1-7321102-5-0

For more information:
info@gettingoutbygoingin.org
Getting Out by Going In,
P.O. Box 88969, Los Angeles, CA, USA 90009

Power Up Your Life
The GOGI Way:

The PowerUp! Manual

*Dedicated to
those who believe prison walls
limit internal freedom...*

*...And to all those who
prove them wrong.*

Preface
By Coach Taylor, GOGI Founder

Getting Out by Going In (GOGI) can be defined as a non-profit organization supporting the expansion of the GOGI Community. That, however, was not how we began, nor is it the limit of our destiny. I remember well the first time a prisoner asked "You mean to get out of prison I need to go inside for the answers?" Getting Out by Going In began as an exploration into solutions for the prisons we humans often create in our own minds.

As GOGI evolved over the years, it became a formal program, then a community, and now "Living the GOGI Way" and "GOGI 4 Life" seem to be in the very vernacular of individuals who were once hopeless and suffered in despair. Now, armed with their GOGI Tools, these individuals are finding their purpose as valued members of society; no longer a deficit but, rather, a great benefit to those who witness their lasting changes. They are leading PowerUp! Community Support Meetings, where like minded individuals can support each other as the solution to problems that erroneously seem too big to manage.

Fueling a movement to replace the worn prison culture of old might have been believed to be impossible, but one prisoner expanded into two who held the vision, then four, then fourteen, then forty, and then the explosive viral nature of GOGI took on a life of its own. Now, it would be impossible to count the number of individuals choosing to PowerUp! as the solution and model their lives The GOGI Way.

Why now? Why this Book?

Support for the growing Culture of GOGI is the reason I wrote Power Up Your Life The GOGI Way: The PowerUp! Manual. Now, with this comprehensive book, an infinite number of individuals who wish to benefit from the daily practice of The GOGI Tools will have all they need to learn, share, and expand the promise of internal freedom.

Please consider this book to be a how-to manual, or like a "Big Book" for GOGI (for those who are familiar with AA). It's like an artist's style guide, or an organizational "bible"; An Ops Manual for those more familiar with procedures outlined in a comprehensive format by large organizations.

This book can be trusted and relied upon as a solid support for the GOGI Culture, as the heart and the soul of this book is consistent with the tens of thousands of individuals who helped form its message.

If you want training and certification options for GOGI Tool study beyond the contents of this book, know that published formal coursework, e-learning options, and supplementary resources are available at www.gettingoutbygoingin.org.

In closing, if you ask me, "What is GOGI?", I am honestly at a loss for words. The GOGI Culture continues to expand and take on new life. There are Bible studies with GOGI tools matching scriptural references. There are AA Meetings with GOGI. There are scientists stating the Tools are nothing more than already-proven behavioral change facts. There are Vets meeting with GOGI to address the concerns of PTSD. There are Muslims reading the Koran and integrating GOGI into their daily life. There are Yoga masters practicing GOGI Yoga. There are body builders practicing Body By GOGI. There is Parenting the GOGI Way, Increasing your Peace Anger Management the GOGI Way, and even the Police Officers Guide to GOGI.

I have NO IDEA what GOGI is. Rather, I should say, I have no idea what GOGI isn't. Living The GOGI Way seems to be in all of us, and when we choose to PowerUp!, it is only then that we find the solution that was within us all along.

With Love,

Coach Taylor
GOGI Founder

Art is a gift to GOGI from GOGI student Sandoval.

The GOGI Tools

Tools of the Body
BOSS OF MY BRAIN

BELLY BREATHING

FIVE SECOND LIGHTSWITCH

Tools of Choice
POSITIVE THOUGHTS

POSITIVE WORDS

POSITIVE ACTIONS

Tools of Moving Forward
CLAIM RESPONSIBILITY

LET GO

FOR–GIVE

Tools of Creation
WHAT IF

REALITY CHECK

ULTIMATE FREEDOM

Table of Contents

The Making of a Miracle
By Coach Taylor, GOGI Founder

At Getting Out by Going In (GOGI), we believe a miracle is made possible even if only one individual has a POSITIVE THOUGHT and stops at nothing to make it a reality for the world to share. The miracle becomes reality when additional people unite and become the solution to the perceived problem. The story behind the creation of the United States' Statue of Liberty beautifully illustrates the possibility of the miracle of freedom in your own life.

Freedom as an Ideal

For some peoples, there will not be an easy connection linking the image of the Statue of Liberty and freedom. The American Indian Nations suffered as a result of the westward expansion, forced off their lands and out of the way of European immigrants building railroads and cities across their homeland. It will not be easy for the decedents of the American Indians to see the Statue of Liberty as a symbol of opportunity for their people.

Similarly, people of the Africa continent suffered as men, women, and children were removed from their land and sold into the slave trade of an emerging nation more than 8,000 miles away. For them, the sting of slavery their ancestors suffered may reverberate in some lives even today.

There were those who suffered in the New World when they became indentured servants, trapped into hard labor and forever in debt to the individual who paid their passage from their homeland to the New World.

Men and women who came to the United States against their will as indentured servants and slaves were forced to leave all they knew, hoping for freedom for their future. They suffered greatly on the open seas before hearing the call from the ship's captain that they had reached land.

For many of these individuals, there could have been

an odd sense of relief that the long journey, sometimes spent entirely in the hull of the ship, was over once they reached land. There must have been great hope for some that one day they, and their people, would gain freedom in this strange new land to which they had been taken. They, too, wanted freedom.

While the Statue of Liberty cannot possibly define the broad spectrum of human experience for all of the incoming immigrants, slaves, indigenous, or the many experiences of exploitation or abuse before the nation developed rules and laws, it does define that aspect of a nation which held the promise of potential. It is to that promise of potential we hope the hurting heart can focus. The intent of the Statue as a symbol of freedom for all mankind can remain undefiled if the reader so wishes.

A Promise of Freedom

My grandmother was only five years old when her family boarded a ship headed for the "New World" in the early 1900s. Leaving Scotland was her father's effort to carve out a life of hope, promise, and prosperity for his family. She told me of the long journey, the rocking of the ship, and the children playing games on the wet and salty deck. She recalled the episodes of seasickness. She recalled the fear she witnessed in adults who were forced to rely on a ship made of wood as they faced thousands of miles of unpredictable ocean.

The final morning of the journey, she heard yelling from a strong Scottish voice on deck as the sun began to rise. "There she is! There she is!" the voice called out, beckoning everyone to come and witness the sight for themselves. At the call, hundreds of immigrants gathered at the side of the ship. Children were lifted onto the shoulders of their weary parents, and all eyes were fixed on the most beautiful image they had ever seen: America's Statue of Liberty.

Tears of joy streamed down the faces of even the most gruff of men. Women tried mostly in vain to teach their children the significance of that one single landmark as they approached American soil. The Statue of Liberty was the undisputed symbol of a miracle for many early immigrants to America and represented the loving arms of a land that would welcome their hard work and effort to build a better life.

The Miracle of the Statue

How America came to own the Statue of Liberty, itself, was quite a miracle. The Statue of Liberty was the idea of the Frenchman, Edouard de Laboulaye, referring to the immigrants headed westward, during a dinner party with friends, "If a monument should rise in the United States, as a memorial to their independence, I should think it only natural if it were built by united effort – a common work of both our nations."

And so, the creation of the gift from the French people to the new lands of America was born out of one man's idea, a POSITIVE THOUGHT, which led to POSITIVE WORDS, leading toward POSITIVE ACTIONS. The statue, created by sculptor, Auguste Bartholdi, with the assistance of Gustave Eiffel, was intended to represent the universal symbol of freedom. It would be the first image greeting hundreds of thousands of immigrants as they completed their voyage across the ocean. The Statue of Liberty was intended as a symbol to signify the ability for anyone who was willing to work to create a new and better life in the New World.

Donations for the Lady

French citizens donated money to create this symbol of freedom and to acknowledge their friendship with America. Hundreds of French laborers worked 10 hours a day for nine years to construct the 350 pieces that were placed into 214 crates for the journey from France to New York.

When the ship with 214 crates arrived, New York City did not have the money needed to pay for the assembly of the statue, and the boxes remained unopened in storage.

Mr. Pulitzer, a citizen and owner of the local newspaper, placed an announcement in the paper suggesting that the citizens not rely on the government and that they pool their donations to erect "Lady Liberty" in the "Land of the Free". It was the people of New York who raised the donations to construct the pedestal and assemble the pieces of Lady Liberty. The cement pedestal was constructed by more than 200 men and was, at the time, the largest concrete structure in the world. Amazingly, the foundation of Lady Liberty remains strong to this day.

Miracles are Possible

The inscription at the base of the statue is a poem by Emma Lazarus, which was written for an auction to raise money to fund Lady Liberty's construction. An excerpt from the poem reads:

Give me your tired, your poor,
Your huddled masses yearning to breathe free,
The wretched refuse of your teeming shore.
Send these, the homeless, tempest-tost to me,
Lift my lamp beside the golden door!

Symbol of Freedom

For more than a 100 years, ships from all over the world made their way into New York Harbor. On every ship, voices were heard exclaiming in every language imaginable, "There is America!," as weary travelers made their way to the side of the ship to witness Lady Liberty for themselves. The sight of Lady Liberty offered hope to many. The miracle of the Statue of Liberty is not only the physical statue. It is also the miracle of the symbol of freedom it represents to the entire world. And, perhaps, most importantly, the achievement that the people of two nations donated their time and money to make the miracle a reality.

How does this Story Relate to You?
How does the symbol of the Statue of Liberty relate to you? Well, you have picked up this book. You may be seeking a new world. And, you may have struggled to leave the old world you experienced behind.

It may seem to you as if you are rowing and rowing in a rickety life boat toward a strange and uncertain future. You may be crossing an ocean of obstacles and pitfalls. This is much like immigrants who left everything they knew with the commitment to make their lives better, or the slaves who were removed from their homes, or even the indentured servants who entered their own form of slavery.

The Vision of GOGI
The vision of GOGI is similar to the vision that gave birth to the Statue of Liberty. Prisoners created GOGI for other prisoners. Volunteers from across the nation gave their time and efforts to make sure the foundation of GOGI was solid and that the GOGI culture was not dependent upon a government, group, or individual.

Donors from across the nation, many of whom were in prison themselves, brought GOGI into reality through their donation of stamps or what little money they could give.

Much like the Statue of Liberty, GOGI, too, is a symbol of the potential within each of us. America was intended to be a land of opportunity for all. It was intended to be the land of miracles, even for you. The GOGI Tools are here to help you create your very own miracle.

GOGI can be a Light in the Dark
May I suggest to you that you bravely enter that strange and uncomfortable world of change with the unwavering faith of early American immigrants. May I suggest that you leave the old behind and face the storms and challenges that will inevitably be standing in your way.

Your GOGI Tools can be your miracle, your personal Statue of Liberty, a light held out to guide you, one that shows you the way, and give you the tools you need to feel welcome in your new world. Much like the volunteers and donors who gifted the Statue of Liberty to America, it was the foundation of volunteers and donations that created The GOGI Tools for you.

My hope is that you are willing to let the light of the GOGI Tools shine within your soul, providing you with a lifetime of internal freedom, which is available to us all.

A Promise to You

The first GOGI book was written as the culmination of one full decade of my work with the incarcerated. By work, I mean my work as the lead volunteer in the GOGI effort. I remember well the first time I entered a prison. It was Federal Correctional Institution, Terminal Island, in San Pedro, California.

I was a Pepperdine University psychology student taking a tour of the drug treatment program at the prison. My instructor, Dr. L. Schoellkopf, was a psychologist for the men at the facility and had arranged for her students to take a tour.

I had never seen a prison and, because I didn't own a television, I had never watched cop shows featuring bad guys in prison. At that time, I had never seen a prison reality show, or even watched "Shawshank Redemption," or other films I would later use to help me learn more about prisoners and why the U.S. was failing our citizens in the "corrections" process of our justice system.

From the first visit to FCI Terminal Island, I felt compelled to view prisons and jails in a manner which differed from popular public opinion. For me, prison was not a place of shame and punishment, but rather, a place of huge opportunity for individuals to become part of the solution.

In 2005, I formed the non-profit organization Getting Out by Going In so I could secure donations of stamps and office supplies with which to respond to mail flooding into our Post Office box.

I also formed the non-profit so an increasing number of volunteers could join "The GOGI Way" of helping prisoners learn a simple way to make positive decisions.

Now, after spending a significant part of my life behind bars as a volunteer, as well as a willing listener and skilled strategist, I can make a few promises to you. I promise if you read this material with an open mind, and if you apply the information each day, you will experience profound changes in every aspect of your life.

I promise you this; your life can become one filled with joy and purpose. Your days can become more enjoyable, your work can become more satisfying, your outlook can become more positive, and your health is likely to improve. And, your GOGI Tools can help.

I can make these promises with confidence because I have seen change in the lives of tens of thousands of incarcerated individuals. Many individuals state that their use of the GOGI Tools was the "missing link" for which they had been searching.

This book was written to encourage you to turn inward, to look within yourself for the answers. All of us at GOGI want you to know that you can "Get Out" of your own internal prison by "Going Inward" for the answers.

All of the answers are within you, just waiting for you to uncover them. My promise is that with GOGI your life can only improve. I am convinced the GOGI Tools just might help unlock the prison which may exist in your mind.

And, once you have created your own internal freedom, then you will experience the joy that comes when you share, by example, how freedom is crafted from within.

With Love,

Coach Taylor
GOGI Founder

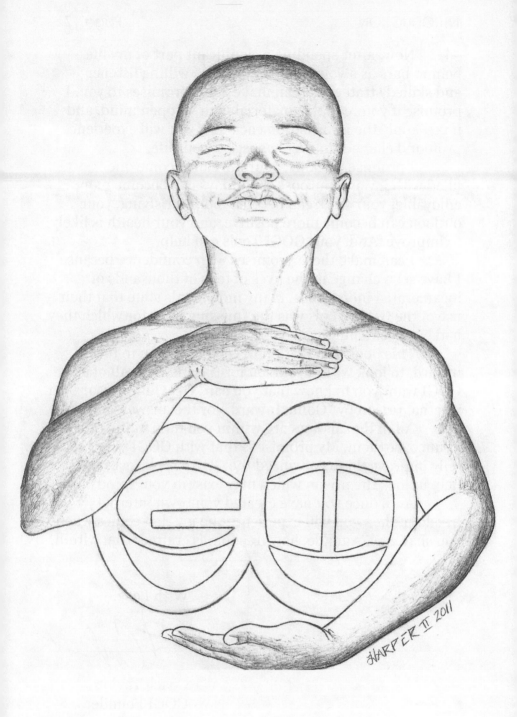

Art is a gift to GOGI from GOGI student Dana Harper.

Section One
The GOGI Tools

———————— Chapter 1 ————————
Getting Out By Going In
GOGI's Humble Beginning

Welcome to the wonderful world of GOGI. What is GOGI, you may ask? Well, at the turn of the century in the early 2000s, I was asking the same question. Actually, my question arose out of a personal dilemma; a feeling of being trapped, stuck, unable to find lasting joy. As a psychology student on a tour of a prison, I was taken aback by how familiar the place looked because the prison looked like how I felt.

Motivated to investigate why this place called prison looked so familiar to my internal life experience, my volunteerism with prisoners began. I became intensely curious about this thing called "freedom" and why some of the prisoners seemed to have more of it than I felt I had ever enjoyed as a free person. Over the subsequent twenty years, thousands of prisoners expressed their perspective of the illusive experience of "freedom" and they eagerly shared with me their opinions on how to get some of it.

Conversations with Prisoners

Conversations with prisoners permitted the discussion to emerge that to get out of prison we must turn inward for the answers. Getting Out by Going In, or "GOGI" as it is affectionately called, was the name given by prisoners who found the simplicity of it's suggested tools helpful.

The words you now read are parts and pieces of tens of thousands of conversations. They are thoughts and reflections written down after large gym-filled seminars as well as small chapel-cramped discussions held in hundreds of different prisons across the United States. They represent the highlights and the lowlights gathered along my often painful journey to the place of internal freedom I enjoy today.

From the Heart and Soul

These words come to you from the heart and soul of the worlds most harm-causing and often the most harmed individuals on our planet as they struggled to earn redemption and the freedom they hoped would follow.

From 2002 until now, their journeys were profoundly intense to witness and occupied much of my life. Through my willingness to listen, and most importantly my willingness to truly hear, during our shared journeys,the prisoners unknowingly delivered to me the key I did not know existed. This key, The GOGI Tools, permitted my own freedom to be found.

While life's circumstances and my own choices never placed me in the custody of a governmental body in charge of keeping others safe, the prison I experienced in my daily living since an early age was not, in my experience, escapable. No one saw my prison. No one understood my prison. I was certain no one felt as I felt. And, I truly believed that no one, not even me, could help.

From where I stood in my life, I believed freedom was simply not to be mine. Believing I was simply born to suffer, I had all but given up – until that day of the prison tour when I saw what I was feeling played out before me in the form of razor wire, block walls, and gun-toting guards.

When I was brave enough, or maybe it was desperate enough, to look within myself for the answers, when I was willing to sit with the suffering individuals among us long enough to explore the "whys" of it all.

That is when the sense of freedom slowly snuck up on me and the doors to a life of satisfaction, joy and contentment was to be mine. It is a journey of getting out of our own prisons by going inward for the answers, and I will forever be grateful to the prisoners who were brave or desperate enough to join me on the journey.

Please Excuse this Book

Please excuse this book for its redundancy. Somehow, on my own journey, I needed these concepts repeated to me a million different ways by thousands of different prisoners before they sunk in long enough to become a habit and eventually be integrated into the very fiber of my daily living. I suspect there are others out there like me who simply don't read well, or who don't comprehend easily, or who just plain can't seem to make knowledge stick

It took one half of a full decade for me to even get a glimpse of what internal freedom might feel like. By then, I had logged more than 10,000 volunteer hours, various forms of freedom and had incessantly asked questions of prisoners. It was in the repetition - including the reading and listening and speaking of the same simple concepts over and over again - that I finally made freedom my reality.

This book is not clever. The concepts are not earth shattering. In fact, you won't find anything new that has not been written or spoken a million times before. What you will find are the same old worn messages you have undoubtedly heard throughout your life. The only difference may be that the message of Getting Out By Going In is delivered with sincerity that comes from suffering; both mine and that of the physical prisoners who joined me in the exploration.

Remember, before you rush to judgment, that I warned you multiple times that there is nothing new about the GOGI Tools. The GOGI Tools are time-proven aids to help you in life, but they are not new. They are not secret. They are not magic. They are not a religion nor are they a club or a cult. The GOGI Tools are not even special.

What are GOGI Tools?

If they are not any of these things, then what are the GOGI Tools? Simply put, the GOGI Tools are simple concepts delivered in an even simpler format that seems to work for a majority of individuals who give them a try. They are free. And, they are for everyone.

In My Own Experience

In my own experience, I found my struggles were not made easier with complex concepts and heavy academic study. My struggles were not aided by scientific proof or well-meaning how-to books. My struggles seemed far too heavy for more heavy stuff to be added to my load. Why wasn't life easier, I wondered? I needed to feel I had control. That I was the boss of my life.

When one prisoner in one of the first volunteer groups commented that I was suggesting that he could be the boss of his brain, the first GOGI Tool was created. BOSS OF MY BRAIN and all subsequent GOGI Tools emerged from conversations with the incarcerated over time.

For me, the concept that I could be the boss of anything empowered me to take charge of what was going on between my two ears. BOSS OF MY BRAIN was added to my toolbox for change. With these words, a prisoner had synthesized ten minutes of my talking about the brain's function, the neurons, and the patterns of behavior into a tool for freedom. He simply chopped away all the unnecessary and delivered up the perfect tool for the job: BOSS OF MY BRAIN.

GOGI and GOGI Tools

In this first section of the book, you will learn about GOGI and the GOGI Tools. For some individuals, it is important to know all the tools in a toolbox. For others, just having one tool and mastery thereof is the winning ticket. The key is to remember there is no wrong and no right way to study the GOGI Tools, as they are simply tools for any individual. Your skill in using one or all of the tools is entirely yours to decide and success will result from your level of commitment and investment.

But, enough about me and the prisoners who were seeking freedom. Let's get to your biggest concern, which is probably you and your life. Let's get started on the path of possibly providing you with a way to shorten your suffering, expedite your freedom, and support you in your quest for satisfaction, contentment, and a life filled with purpose and meaning.

On the following pages, you are provided with basic answers to many of the questions initially asked by inquisitive minds. Hopefully this section will resolve questions that are likely to emerge. If some things do not apply, please muscle forward through the material until that morsel of wisdom or encouragement you desire makes itself known.

Please know you are appreciated for investing your time in these words. My hope is that the value of your time and money exceeds your greatest expectation and you come to realize how simple the experience of freedom can become when we choose to get out by going in.

Could GOGI be Your Solution?

Like most of us, there were times in my life when I felt trapped, stuck, and locked into what seemed to be a prison for which I had no key. The hopelessness I felt about my own life reverberated into my daily choices, which further embedded me into a life over which I felt no control.

As a psychology student on a tour of a prison, I was struck by how familiar the prison yard looked. In an odd and somewhat indescribable way, there was a sense of familiarity in the drab buildings, impenetrable walls, and guards with guns ready to remind me of my unfortunate position in life. The prison looked like how I felt inside. I, too, felt as if my life was a prison from which there was no escape.

On that day, I became committed to the exploration of freedom. What was freedom? How did it feel? And, most importantly, how could I get some of it? For the answers, I turned towards those wearing prison uniforms, as no one on the "outside" seemed to provide an acceptable answer for the sense of worthlessness, hopelessness, and despair I experienced as my daily existence.

Tiny Doses of Freedom

Nearly twenty years later, I am relieved to share with you that along the journey as a volunteer working with prisoners, my freedom was gained in sometimes imperceptible increments. It almost seemed as if tiny doses of freedom were released into my life experience through my deliberate choices, each decision adding to the ocean of possibilities which became the life I now enjoy. This freedom I created in my life was not immediate, nor was it because someone other than me gave me permission to be free. Rather, I got out of my prison by going inward for the answers.

The prisoners taught me this; that my freedom was mine to plant, nurture and grow within me. And, in doing so over a sustained period of time, I would experience an uncommon level of internal freedom that could not be negatively impacted by circumstance or situation. The internal freedom available to me could not and would not be contained, but only if I remained deliberate and dedicated to my quest for freedom.

In my heart, I feel it is now time the GOGI journey of Getting Out By Going Inward can be shared with society. Why now? Of this I am certain; in a very real way, many prisoners seem to be more free than those who live outside of a physical prison, those who appear to have all the freedom in the world.

The Message

The message within these pages comes to you from time spent with tens of thousands of prisoners who helped create, develop and now share a set of simple decision making tools they have found to be helpful on the journey to internal freedom. These Tools are now available to you, as a gift from those whose prison walls of regret, remorse, addiction, gangs, and criminal lifestyles were seemingly impossible to reconcile. Know that prisons come in all forms and are not only for those who break the rules. Sometimes, the internal prisons are more difficult to perceive as anything less than a life sentence.

This book shares the knowledge gleaned on the journey of GOGI students and is intended for all people, even for "free" people. It is a gift from prisoners who helped create this information I can now offer.

The hope of all GOGI students is that physically "free" people find internal freedom without the painful journey that defined their own lives behind bars.

The Tools shared in this book may have been created by some of the most harmful and the most harmed in our society, but if these Tools helped many of them evolve into providing solutions for their communities. Wouldn't it stand to reason these Tools may help you, too?

How Can This Book Help You?

This book can help you if you:

1) Have tried. If you have tried other methods for change but none of them seem to last, this book might provide a little nudge in the right direction.
2) Are tired. If you are tired of trying and you simply want change, and if you are just about willing to do anything to get a different outcome, this book might give you a solid route.
3) Are motivated. If you are motivated for change but have not yet found that "spark" of excitement in the same old methods, this book might light that fire.
4) Are curious. If you enjoy expanding your knowledge about all sorts of things, you may find this book very interesting.
5) Are helpful. If you are helpful to others on the journey of change, it is likely you will find the information in this book supportive of your efforts.
6) Are in any other state of flux. If you are in-between where you were and where you want to be, then this book may help you create a bit more distance from the unwanted.

Here's What You Will Find

In this book you will be introduced to the Getting Out by Going In (GOGI) organization, as well as how it has evolved as a lifestyle. You will have the ability to learn about the GOGI Calendar of Study, PowerUp! Community Meetings, as well as the specifics of the four Sets of Tools and instructions to use each of the Tools.

The goal of this book is to provide you with Tools you can use to increase your positive decision making and maximize your life experience.

GOGI

Art is a gift to GOGI from GOGI student R. Ojeda.

─────── Chapter 2 ───────
The GOGI Tools

How might your ability to make positive decisions be increased with your use of simple Tools? The more you read about and study the GOGI Tools, the more you may find them helpful in every decision you make from this day forward.

For this reason, information about the tools is repeated in many different ways, just to make sure you have maximum opportunity to put them to good use.

What are The GOGI Tools?

The GOGI Tools are based on common and well-known psychological and behavioral techniques. There is nothing new about the Tools, but somehow the simple description of the Tools makes them easier to remember and apply.

Simplifying otherwise complex strategies has been the most important aspect of GOGI's positive decision making Tools. It is the foundation of GOGI's incredible success in providing anyone who is interested with a viable option for lasting change.

GOGI is Keeping it Simple

Simplicity is sometimes the most overlooked value in our society. Individuals and societies make the mistake of thinking lasting change needs to be complex, scientific, and rigorously proven. GOGI, however, is successful because the Tools are based on nothing more than the fact that they are simple and they work. If that is a bit too simple, then the number of success stories may eventually sway the naysayer's mind. We keep it simple and let practice over time prove it.

GOGI = Simple Resource

Those of us who study the GOGI Tools know the lasting power of any change is dependent upon the individual's ability and commitment to utilizing every possible resource to support that change. The GOGI Tools just happen to be a simple and easy-to-apply resource.

If more people would appreciate living a simple life, using simple Tools, and keeping their mind uncluttered, our prisons and jails, as well as our pharmacies and doctor's offices, would have huge "vacancy" signs.

While often understated, simple is sometimes the most powerful choice you can make. Yes, the GOGI Tools are simple by design. Change can be simple, too, when you increase your ability to make positive decisions. You can do this through your use of the GOGI Tools.

The GOGI Tools

Tools of the Body
BOSS OF MY BRAIN

BELLY BREATHING

FIVE SECOND LIGHTSWITCH

Tools of Choice
POSITIVE THOUGHTS

POSITIVE WORDS

POSITIVE ACTIONS

Tools of Moving Forward
CLAIM RESPONSIBILITY

LET GO

FOR–GIVE

Tools of Creation
WHAT IF

REALITY CHECK

ULTIMATE FREEDOM

Tools of the Body

BOSS OF MY BRAIN is part of the set of Tools called TOOLS OF THE BODY. This was the first Tool created by GOGI students as they explored ways to make certain they remained on track with the kind of life they wanted. By identifying the SMART PART, the EMOTIONAL PART and the OLD HABIT PART, you can simplify the process of controlling how your brain operates. When you use this Tool frequently enough, you will begin to experience the power that comes with practice. BOSS OF MY BRAIN solves the problem of not being taught by example or by education that you and only you are the owner of the business of your brain. No one else is living your exact life and with BOSS OF MY BRAIN, you can now run the business of your life just like a good boss runs a good company.

BELLY BREATHING is part of the set of Tools called TOOLS OF THE BODY and was created when a group of GOGI students tried to explain to a young student how to get out of the loop of automatic thinking. In a Peer Mentor Circle, the GOGI students asked the youngster to lay on the ground, looking up at the ceiling until his belly began to move with every breath. This is a simple trick you can try every night when you lay down to sleep. Just lay on your back until your belly starts to move. You don't need to even think about breathing with your belly moving because it will happen on its own. When your belly begins to move, that is when you are BELLY BREATHING. When you notice you are using your Tool BELLY BREATHING, you can focus on doing it even when you are standing.

FIVE SECOND LIGHTSWITCH is part of the set of Tools called TOOLS OF THE BODY and was created when a group of GOGI students wanted to find a way to get their actions to not be so reactive or automatic. Wanting to find a way to simply stop decisions and choices that are lightning fast and seemed out of control, they created the ability to FLIP THE SWITCH and redirect any thought to a positive action within five seconds. When you have a positive action already picked out, it is easier to FLIP that FIVE SECOND LIGHTSWITCH you have ready and make sure you don't make the same mistakes from the past. FLIP THE SWITCH and you can shine the light where you are directing your life, and go that direction with confidence.

Tools of Choice

POSITIVE THOUGHTS is part of the set of Tools called TOOLS OF CHOICE and was created when a group of GOGI Girls were in a small housing module, day in and day out, with very little ability to get away from each other for much needed alone time. Being in a situation where alone time was not possible, they created this Tool to build their ability to withstand all sorts of peer pressure, bad attitudes, drug and alcohol addiction, and general negativity. Being in a very difficult situation, they decided that rather than to give up and give in, they would become even more committed to living positive lives. You can do this, too, with POSITIVE THOUGHTS. When negativity creeps into your head, you can banish it forever with your fix-it Tool called POSITIVE THOUGHTS.

POSITIVE WORDS is part of the set of Tools called TOOLS OF CHOICE and was created by the GOGI Girls when they realized that it was not enough to simply use POSITIVE THOUGHTS. They quickly realized that if their thoughts remained in their head, they were vulnerable to outside influence. When they used their POSITIVE WORDS, it was almost as if they were building an additional shield of protection to keep from being negatively impacted, regardless of the outside circumstances. When they used POSITIVE WORDS, they were less inclined to become the victim of negative circumstances. You can use your POSITIVE WORDS as your biggest weapon to fend off attackers of your peace of mind and positive life.

POSITIVE ACTIONS is part of the set of Tools called TOOLS OF CHOICE. This tool was the obvious Tool emerging from the other TOOLS OF CHOICE. This is because the GOGI Girls realized that it was possible to shield yourself from negative by using POSITIVE THOUGHTS and they would increase their protection by POSITIVE WORDS, but when they used POSITIVE ACTIONS they drove away people, places, and things that did not positively support what they wanted in life. With practice, you can use POSITIVE ACTIONS to prove to yourself and others that it IS possible to change the course of your life and be happy, positive, sober/sane, and successful.

Tools of Moving Forward

CLAIM RESPONSIBILITY is part of the set of Tools called TOOLS OF MOVING FORWARD. This Tool is not about claiming responsibility for the past. Instead, the Tool CLAIM RESPONSIBILITY is about today and tomorrow. When you use this Tool, you realize that how you respond and react to anyone or anything is under your direct command. No one can make you angry. It is you who gets to choose if you will let others anger you. No one can make you violent. It is you who gets to choose if you will let others bring out violence in your behavior. No one can make you drink or use drugs. It is you who gets to choose if you put yourself in a position where saying no is a challenge. When you use CLAIM RESPONSIBILITY, you move forward, toward the life that you may never have thought possible.

LET GO is part of the set of Tools called TOOLS OF MOVING FORWARD and was created for people who have a tendency to carry the heavy load of their past with them into the present and the future. By putting negative thoughts about people, places and things in your hand, and giving them the HAND/SQUASH/TOSS, you will find there is more room in your head and your heart for more positive life choices. To actually be a better person, you move forward beyond the heavy darkness intruding in your decisions today. Regret is essential, but wallowing in regret so long that it makes for other poor decisions is just not smart. Give it the HAND/SQUASH/TOSS and commit to using LET GO so you can move forward and make more positive choices.

FOR-GIVE is part of the set of Tools called TOOLS OF MOVING FORWARD. In truth, this is the GOGI "safety" Tool. This Tool gives you permission to get a safe distance from harmful people, places and things. When you are under attack or in danger, you will become selfish and uncaring. As a safety Tool, FOR-GIVE has you asking what you need to do to get a safe distance from harm. In asking that question, you are putting yourself in a position to be a benefit to yourself, your family, friends and community. When you are safe from harm, you will undoubtedly begin to give back to others. FOR you to GIVE you must be "SAFE FROM HARM". Get safe, then, give back with your handy Tool FOR-GIVE.

Tools of Creation

WHAT IF is part of the set of Tools called TOOLS OF CREATION. This Tool lets you create new outcomes for yourself by taking you out of life's victim seat and putting you in charge of your decisions. You can give everything the WHAT IF all day, every day so you can see just where your choices are leading you. WHAT IF you signed up for a class? WHAT if you didn't? WHAT IF you made that phone call? WHAT IF you didn't? WHAT IF you reached out to someone in need? WHAT IF you didn't? When you WHAT IF all your choices, you will find that most of your choices today are exactly the same as your choices yesterday. How are you expecting a different outcome with the same choices? With this Tool you can give all thoughts, words and actions the WHAT IF and create something different from the past.

REALITY CHECK is part of the set of Tools called TOOLS OF CREATION. This Tool is your permission to be a flawed human, but does not give you permission to remain in a flawed state. "TEN STEPS FORWARD AND TWO STEPS BACK is still EIGHT STEPS AHEAD." Your two steps back do not mean you are a failure. What it means, when you use REALITY CHECK, is that you acknowledge you really messed up. You get right back on track by making your very next decision be the most positive decision possible. With REALITY CHECK, you understand that you are not perfect, but you keep moving forward towards perfection with your next thought, word, and action. Your mistakes do not define you, what defines you is how you get back on track once mistakes are made. REALITY CHECK lets you course-correct quickly.

ULTIMATE FREEDOM is part of the set of Tools called TOOLS OF CREATION. This Tool is the least obvious of the Tools because it is used to create a way of moving through your day and not necessarily a tool you pull out when something breaks down. When you use your Tool ULTIMATE FREEDOM, you are deciding that your decisions are helping you be of service. You do this by being positive; that is a service to others. You do this by being helpful; that is a service to others. You do this by being a safe distance from harm; that is a service to others. When you use ULTIMATE FREEDOM, you realize that you are important as a walking, talking potential solution to any and every problem. As a walking and talking solution, you are living a life of service. THAT is the ultimate use of the Tool ULTIMATE FREEDOM.

A gift to GOGI from an anonymous student.

My signature _____ ID number _____

Print your name Francisco Padilla Location N.K.S.P

GOGI Calendar of Study

The GOGI week starts on a Monday. Where there is a 5th Monday in the month, review all Tools.

JANUARY
Week 1 BOSS OF MY BRAIN

Week 2 BELLY BREATHING

Week 3 FIVE SECOND LIGHTSWITCH

Week 4 POSITIVE THOUGHTS

FEBRUARY
Week 1 POSITIVE WORDS

Week 2 POSITIVE ACTIONS

Week 3 CLAIM RESPONSIBILITY

Week 4 LET GO

MARCH
Week 1 FOR--GIVE

Week 2 WHAT IF

Week 3 REALITY CHECK

Week 4 ULTIMATE FREEDOM

APRIL
Week 1 BOSS OF MY BRAIN

Week 2 BELLY BREATHING

Week 3 FIVE SECOND LIGHTSWITCH

Week 4 POSITIVE THOUGHTS

MAY
Week 1 POSITIVE WORDS

Week 2 POSITIVE ACTIONS

Week 3 CLAIM RESPONSIBILITY

Week 4 LET GO

JUNE
Week 1 FOR--GIVE

Week 2 WHAT IF

Week 3 REALITY CHECK

Week 4 ULTIMATE FREEDOM

JULY
Week 1 BOSS OF MY BRAIN

Week 2 BELLY BREATHING

Week 3 FIVE SECOND LIGHTSWITCH

Week 4 POSITIVE THOUGHTS

AUGUST
Week 1 POSITIVE WORDS

Week 2 POSITIVE ACTIONS

Week 3 CLAIM RESPONSIBILITY

Week 4 LET GO

SEPTEMBER
Week 1 FOR--GIVE

Week 2 WHAT IF

Week 3 REALITY CHECK

Week 4 ULTIMATE FREEDOM

OCTOBER
Week 1 BOSS OF MY BRAIN

Week 2 BELLY BREATHING

Week 3 FIVE SECOND LIGHTSWITCH

Week 4 POSITIVE THOUGHTS

NOVEMBER
Week 1 POSITIVE WORDS

Week 2 POSITIVE ACTIONS

Week 3 CLAIM RESPONSIBILITY

Week 4 LET GO

DECEMBER
Week 1 FOR--GIVE

Week 2 WHAT IF

Week 3 REALITY CHECK

Week 4 ULTIMATE FREEDOM

The GOGI Tool Guide

Tools Of The Body

BOSS OF MY BRAIN

The Three Parts:
Smart Part
Emotional Part
Old Habit Part

Which one is the boss
right now?

BELLY BREATHING

Feel The Flow:

One hand on my chest.
One hand on my belly.

Which hand is moving?

FIVE SECOND LIGHTSWITCH

Old Thought?
New Action.
I have an OLD THOUGHT
and I have a NEW ACTION
By the count of 5
I get to my NEW ACTION.

Tools Of Choice

POSITIVE THOUGHTS

Is it Powerful?
Is it Productive?
Is it Positive?

With every thought,
I ask the 3 P's.

POSITIVE WORDS

Is it Powerful?
Is it Productive?
Is it Positive?

With every word,
I ask the 3 P's.

POSITIVE ACTIONS

Is it Powerful?
Is it Productive?
Is it Positive?

With every action,
I ask the 3 P's.

The GOGI Tool Guide

Tools Of Moving Forward	Tools Of Creation
CLAIM RESPONSIBILITY	**WHAT IF**
Am I Proud of this Choice? I am responsible for all my actions and all my reactions today.	**What if I am not my past?** No to the past = Yes to the future.
LET GO	**REALITY CHECK**
Hand/Squash/Toss When bothered, I put the feelings in my hand, squash it, and toss it away from me.	**Ten and Two Rule** Ten steps forward and two steps back is still eight steps ahead.
FOR–GIVE	**ULTIMATE FREEDOM**
For me to Give I need distance from harm. For me to give, I unhook from the past, and find my internal freedom.	**Being Free is up to me.** Living a life of service sets me free.

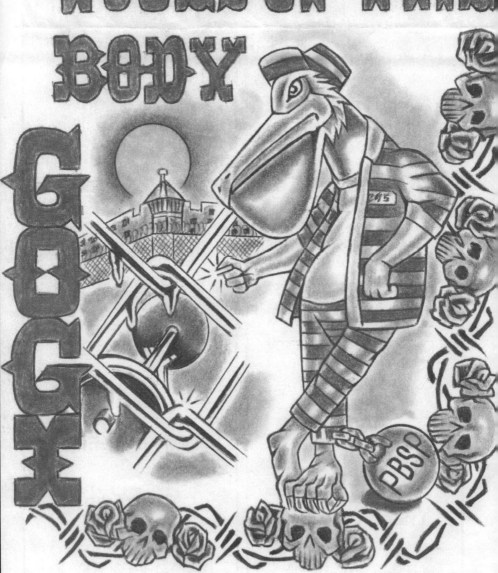

—————— Chapter 3 ——————
The Tools of the Body

BOSS OF MY BRAIN
BELLY BREATHING
FIVE SECOND LIGHTSWITCH

The tools in this section are THE TOOLS OF THE BODY. They are designed to help you master the machine of your body. If you make a practice of using these tools, you will find yourself making positive decisions more often.

The TOOLS OF THE BODY empower you to control your human body. TOOLS OF THE BODY let you formulate positive decisions as a result of having control over your body's reaction to challenges.

These Tools help you learn how much power you have over your body and its seemingly automatic operation.

The biggest challenge in applying these Tools as an adult could be that you didn't use them as a child. Your decisions of the past probably would have been different had you known about GOGI Tools.

With BOSS OF MY BRAIN, BELLY BREATHING and FIVE SECOND LIGHTSWITCH, you take control over your choices.

In this section, you will explore the most frequently referred to set of GOGI Tools, and, coincidentally, the first set of tools created by prisoners. The TOOLS OF THE BODY are as simple as the name suggests, enabling the individual a level of mastery of the mind, breathing, and redirecting attention.

In my own life, these tools helped me build a solid foundation from which all other positive decision making tools could be practiced. For me, the TOOLS OF THE BODY placed the locus of control squarely in my hands and forevermore it became impossible for me to play the victim or blame anyone else for my outcomes.

BOSS OF MY BRAIN

When I learned BOSS OF MY BRAIN, I realized that sadness, depression, and anxiety could be perceived as choices just like appreciation, hope, and gratitude. I realized that my life experience was mine to create and that BOSS OF MY BRAIN is an awesome tool in helping me create a life I actually enjoyed. That is when the use of this tool became almost second nature, simply because of the relief I experienced. I wanted more joy and less pain in my life and BOSS OF MY BRAIN helped me get closer to those goals.

BELLY BREATHING

BELLY BREATHING provides me with a powerful resource of energy and intention as I am returned to a state of deliberate living rather than reactionary responses. When I began to utilize BELLY BREATHING as a way I simply lived every day, that is when my life opened up not only to deliberate living, but living with appreciation for challenges I could now let slide by me with little disruption to my focus.

FIVE SECOND LIGHTSWITCH

Fortified with my FIVE SECOND LIGHTSWITCH, there is nothing that stays in my way long enough to take me off my intended outcome. At any moment, I can flip my switch and shine a bright light on any situation. This is because I am now in charge of how long I permit a thought to linger. If I am in some way unhappy, then it is only me who can choose to flip that switch and neurologically move that thought to a more powerful one.

Using the TOOLS OF THE BODY is a skill that can be mastered in childhood. A child who learns these tools before the age of eight is well poised to navigate the next phase of development with the grace and ease we all wish represented our childhoods. From birth to nearly eight years of age, children are learning to master their bodies, learning to make decisions, and learning to make choices that have outcomes from which they benefit or suffer. TOOLS OF THE BODY empower children to realize they have significant control over their life, even while at the mercy of their caregivers.

Kids Get GOGI

One of my fondest GOGI memories is of my day spent in a Compton, California middle school. The principal permitted the GOGI Coaches to work with a small group of kids to see what they thought about the GOGI Tools. The teachers were instructed to send one student from each class out to meet with a GOGI Coach. As luck would have it, we were assigned those kids the teachers wanted to get out of their classrooms due to the disruptive nature of their personalities. That was fine by us, as we figured the GOGI Tools would not work fully if they did not work in the most difficult of situations.

"Hey kids," I said over the growing volume of voices coming from the small group of boys now seated at the picnic table. "One voice and let it be mine for a minute."

The group of eight rowdy boys looked up towards me with anticipation as I stood sure-footed at the head of the table. They had gotten out of class and saw the entire playground calling to them. I knew I had about five seconds before their attention span was stretched to the limit.

"Who knows how an A student sits in a classroom? Do any of you know how an A student sits in a classroom?" I asked.

Nearly all the kids, following the little shot caller's lead, sat up straight and put their hands folded on the top of the table.

"So, that is how an A student sits at this school?" I asked.

With a couple of nods as my reply, I continued.

You are the Boss

"Right now you all are the boss. That is so cool. Each one of you is using the SMART part of your brain to be the boss of your own brain and be like A students. You are using BOSS OF MY BRAIN as your tool without even knowing it. That is so, so cool. If you continue to do this good while I am here, then I want to call the principal out here and show her that each of you can act like an A student when you use BOSS OF MY BRAIN."

They smiled, and kept their A-student position as if yearning for more compliments.

"Ok. Let's see how you do with the next tool. Follow me," I said, as I walked over to the side of a school building with my little crew following in eager anticipation as if I was handing out candy or some other reward for their inevitable accomplishment.

"BELLY BREATHING. That is our next tool. When you use BELLY BREATHING, you are getting oxygen to your brain, which makes your decisions smarter. Without oxygen to your brain, you do not make your smartest decisions. Who here has made smart decisions?" I asked.

All the hands went up.

"And who here has made some pretty dumb decisions?"

All hands stayed up.

"Well, if you were using your Tool BELLY BREATHING, there is no way you would have made dumb decisions, because BELLY BREATHING gets oxygen to your brain. What did I say about oxygen to your brain?" I asked, hoping at least one of them was listening.

"It's makes us smarter," Delvonte belted out.

"Exactly!," I replied.

Run the Fence Line

"Ok. We are going to practice BELLY BREATHING. See that fence down there?" I pointed to the fence about 50 feet away." We are going to run to the end of the fence and back. On your mark. Get set. Go!"

The kids took off like bolts of lightning, returning back as quickly as their middle-school feet could get them there. Gathering around me like little baby chicks, they waited for my next morsel of whatever it was that was making them feel pretty good about themselves.

"Put your hand on your belly. Put your other hand on your chest. Which one is moving? Your belly? Or your chest?" I asked.

"Belly," they replied almost in unison.

"Great. Now is the time to make decisions. Your belly is moving. You are using your Tool BELLY BREATHING. That is when you want to make your decisions, when your belly is moving in and out. That is BELLY BREATHING and that is when you make your best decisions. Tell me a good decision you can make right now?"

"I'm gunna run faster next time," one said.

"I'm gunna sit like an A student," said another.

"I won't yell at my brother," said a third.

Great Decisions

"Great decisions," I replied. "You are all being the boss and now you are making smart decisions because you are getting oxygen to your brain. Great work."

"Let's do it again." One of the boys added.

The boys eagerly complied and ran back and forth, automatically placing their hand on their chest and belly upon return.

"Look, my belly is moving," one said.

"Mine, too," another chimed in.

I walked away and sure enough the little crew was hot on my heels, excited they were learning how powerful they were and how good they were at these things called the GOGI Tools.

"Next, we need to test your ability to flip your FIVE SECOND LIGHTSWITCH. Do you want to see if you can do this Tool, too?" It was unanimous.

After listening quite attentively to the key words of

the Tool and how they can flip the switch and move to a positive action, we were ready. We staged three scenarios with which the boys could relate. One was mouthing off to a teacher. One was a bully on the yard. The other was not listening at home. The boys created an impromptu skit for each scenario.

The Rambunctious Student

The first skit portrayed a situation with which the boys were obviously familiar. One boy played the teacher; the other, the rambunctious student. The teacher in the skit asked the boy to sit down and the boy was going to mouth off. Instead, he flipped his FIVE SECOND LIGHTSWITCH and made a more positive choice. It took several tries but through several minutes of nervous laughter, the skit was complete and the scenario was played out to a positive outcome. The two boys in the skit received a round of applause.

Bully on the Yard

Next up was the "bully on the yard" scenario, which, thankfully, went a bit smoother than the first, and was taken a bit more seriously. Another round of applause for the "bully on the yard" skit.

Mother at Home

And finally, the mother at home skit. None of the boys wanted to play the mother so they assigned me. That skit, earned its fair share of applause.

"You boys are excellent at these GOGI Tools. You know you have BOSS OF MY BRAIN. You can always use BELLY BREATHING. And, to top it off, you can flip your FIVE SECOND LIGHTSWITCH any time you are being pushed to the edge," I said in a brief recap as our time together was coming to a close.

"We need to tell our friends!," one of the boys blurted out.

This was confirmation to me of the beauty of the

GOGI Tools. Once learned, I have yet to meet a person who wants to squirrel them away. People, even little middle schoolers, want to share their GOGI Tools.

Take it to the Classrooms

After a brief recap, it didn't take too long to seek out and gain permission from the principal to bring the boys into one of the classrooms to have them report on their GOGI Tools. Other than the occasional nudge in the right direction, I let the boys share their Tools. The kids laughed. The teacher laughed. I marveled at how these little outcasts and perceived problem children could be so driven to share their tools with their peers. I asked the classroom of kids how many of them believed they were their own boss and they all raised their hands. I congratulated the GOGI boys and encouraged all students to remember they are always the boss of their own brain.

End of a Compton Kind of Day

With that, my day at the Compton Middle School ended. There would not likely be a miracle that created A-students out of a 2-hour GOGI workshop, of that I was certain. Change, lasting change, takes practice, positive reinforcement, and repetition. But, what was obvious was the hunger for simple, positive decision making tools among those once perceived to be the teachers' most difficult students.

Tools of the Body

TOOLS OF THE BODY are ideal for the eight-year-old in all of us, that part of us that often fails to remember our power, our innate right, and our responsibility to direct our lives to our greatest satisfaction.

The heart of GOGI
brings forth all good things.

Art is a gift to GOGI from GOGI student Henry J. Coots.

—————— Chapter 4 ——————
The GOGI Tool
BOSS OF MY BRAIN

BOSS OF MY BRAIN is part of the set of Tools called TOOLS OF THE BODY. This was the first Tool created by GOGI students as they explored ways to make certain they remained on track with the kind of life they wanted. By identifying the SMART PART, the EMOTIONAL PART and the OLD HABIT PART, you can simplify the process of controlling how your brain operates. When you use this Tool frequently enough, you will begin to experience the power that comes with practice. BOSS OF MY BRAIN solves the problem of not being taught by example or education that you and only you are the owner of the business of your brain. No one else is living your exact life and with BOSS OF MY BRAIN you can now run the business of your life just like a good boss runs a good company.

The truth of the matter is you are the boss of everything that goes on in your mind and with this tool you are provided the ability to understand just how simple mastery can become.

With BOSS OF MY BRAIN, we break down the complex function of the brain into very simplistic components. In GOGI, there are three areas of the brain you need in order to understand how to use BOSS OF MY BRAIN. The SMART PART of your brain is right behind your forehead. You have the EMOTIONAL PART and which is at the very center of your brain. You have an OLD HABIT PART and that is at the very back of the brain, where your neck and head meet.

We often let our EMOTIONAL PART and OLD

HABIT PART dictate our lives. We get emotional and react in an old habit manner. Sometimes we fail to use the SMART PART of our brain to make sense of our emotions and old habits.

When we focus on the SMART PART of our brain, we realize the power we gave up in our past is actually power we can take back today. Using the Tool BOSS OF MY BRAIN allows you to decide which part of your brain you want to have the contro, the SMART PART, EMOTIONAL PART, or OLD HABIT PART. After all, you are the boss.

You only have three parts of your brain that need your management and the Tool BOSS OF MY BRAIN gives you control over all three. You can think smart, think emotionally, or think from a series of old habits. You are the boss, even if you have not been a good boss in the past, you can be a good boss now. No one is boss over your brain but you. If you want to manage your mind more effectively, then BOSS OF MY BRAIN is the Tool you can use.

The truth is, you have a brain that is yours and yours alone. It is exclusively your brain and will operate under your instruction, or your lack of instruction. No one can control your brain unless you give them permission or leave your brain so unattended or drug-impaired that others can walk right into your thought process and start filling your brain with garbage.

Still, even if you give your brain over to someone or something else, it is yours to give over. You have a brain and you are the boss, even if you are a lazy boss.

A Good Boss is Attentive

In any business, being a good boss means you are attentive, you want top performance, and you know how to care for the company's goals and objectives. When you use your GOGI Tool and claim your ownership by using BOSS OF MY BRAIN, you are declaring that no one, no situation, and no circumstance has control over your ability to control your brain.

You can be told to stand in a line, but you can't be told what to think while standing. You and only you are the boss of every thought you create.

That being said, to be the best boss, we have simplified the process with the use of the GOGI Tool BOSS OF MY BRAIN. We have found that individuals who often suffer from depression, sadness, hopelessness and even rage and anger like this GOGI Tool.

This is because for the very first time, in some cases, they realize they are in control no matter how out of control their brain seems. This Tool gives just enough power to grab hold of your thinking and create a new possibility.

No matter how fried or how fermented you believe your brain may be, there are always new, fresh, clean and ready brain cells being created inside your brain just waiting for your instructions. It is never too late to use BOSS OF MY BRAIN to take control of your life.

Gustavo Fernandez

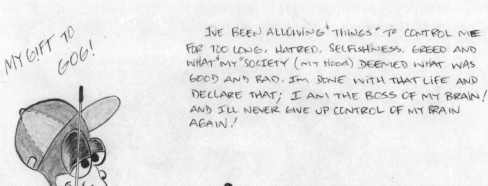

IVE BEEN ALLOWING "THINGS" TO CONTROL ME FOR TOO LONG, HATRED, SELFISHNESS, GREED AND WHAT "MY" SOCIETY (MY HOOD) DEEMED WHAT WAS GOOD AND BAD. IM DONE WITH THAT LIFE AND DECLARE THAT; I AM THE BOSS OF MY BRAIN! AND ILL NEVER GIVE UP CONTROL OF MY BRAIN AGAIN!

BOSS OF MY BRAIN
THE THREE PARTS
Smart Part
Emotional Part
Old Habit Part

Which part is the boss right now?

To effectively use BOSS OF MY BRAIN, remember: there are three parts of your brain:

- The SMART PART of your brain in the front.
- The EMOTIONAL PART of your brain in the middle.
- The OLD HABIT PART of your brain in the back.

To use BOSS OF MY BRAIN, simply ask yourself, "Which part of my brain is in charge right now?".

When you ask yourself this question, you are using BOSS OF MY BRAIN.

If you do nothing more, if you read no further, if you learn nothing more than this tool, your life can change for the better. You ARE the boss. No one can make you mad or make you act any certain way. YOU can choose to let something make you mad, but no one can do that for you. No one can control your brain unless you give them permission to be boss over your brain.

♥~ *Coach Taylor*

Chapter 5
The **GOGI** Tool
BELLY BREATHING

BELLY BREATHING is part of the set of Tools called TOOLS OF THE BODY and was created when a group of GOGI students tried to explain to a young student how to get out of the loop of automatic thinking. In a Peer-Mentor circle, the GOGI students asked the youngster to lay on the ground and look up at the ceiling until his belly began to move with every breath. This is a simple trick you can try every night when you lay down to sleep, just lay on your back until your belly starts to move.

You don't need to even think about breathing with your belly moving because it will happen on its own. When your belly begins to move, that is when you are BELLY BREATHING. When you notice you are using your Tool BELLY BREATHING, you can focus on doing it even when you are standing.

Your body is designed so that oxygen is transported by your blood to every part of your body. If you observe others, you will notice that most people breathe with shallow breath. You will see their chest move up and down. What you won't see is their belly moving in and out with every breath.

BELLY BREATHING is a Tool you can use to return to your optimal breath, even if a majority of other individuals don't breathe properly. Just because everybody is doing something, does not make it right. Most people forgot how to breathe early on in their lives and consequently they are quick to anger, not as smart with decisions as they could be, and are less healthy than they could be if they would just practice the GOGI Tool BELLY BREATHING.

If you want to see if you are BELLY BREATHING, simply put a hand on your chest and a hand on your belly. Which one moves the most? If you are BELLY BREATHING, your belly will move and your chest won't.

Here is an interesting fact: It is nearly impossible to be in rage or out of control with anger and use the GOGI Tool BELLY BREATHING at the same time. If you want to learn to be peaceful inside and react, even to stressful situations, in a calm manner, BELLY BREATHING is a great Tool.

If you were to watch a baby breathe, it would seem as if their entire body was involved in the breathing process. In truth, that is how we humans are designed to breathe, with our entire bodies. When we are breathing in a relaxed manner, our entire body is benefiting from oxygen getting to every bit of our bloodstream.

The problem is, quite early on, we unlearn our breathing. If you walk a prison yard, you will see that many of the individuals have their hands balled up almost into fists. And, more importantly, if you watch their breathing you will not see their stomach area moving in and out naturally. Rather, you will see their chest move when they breathe. These individuals are not optimally getting oxygen into their bodies.

No More Fight or Flight

When we do not get oxygen to our bodies, we often are in or get into a "fight or flight" way of thinking. We often anger more quickly, we are short tempered, we don't think clearly, and we are reactionary. Breathing with the entire body is one of the most powerful ways to calm the body and the mind. It is the finest way to diffuse a fight or rationally control thoughts of anger or rage. BELLY BREATHING as a GOGI Tool is a powerful sign of self-control, self-awareness, and maturity.

The GOGI students who tend to rely greatly on BELLY BREATHING as their "go to" Tool are often those students who claim to be reactionary, defensive, argumentative, opinionated, or stubborn. They report that the GOGI Tool, BELLY BREATHING, has kept them from flying off the handle, overreacting, or making a mistake which could add time to their stay in an undesirable gated community.

BELLY BREATHING is designed to get you into the habit of breathing like your body was meant to breathe. Remember, it is never too late. You have a lot of breathing left to do.

Breathe Like the Shaolin

The most famous temple in China is the Shaolin Monastery, where Monks train their entire lives in the art of breathing. Through mastery of the breath they learn to endure and ultimately conquer the internal as well as the external enemies. The Shaolin Monks understand that without control of the breath, there is little control over anything else. Using your BELLY BREATHING Tool, you can endure and eventually conquer the inevitable challenges in your life. You can be like the Shaolin when you master BELLY BREATHING.

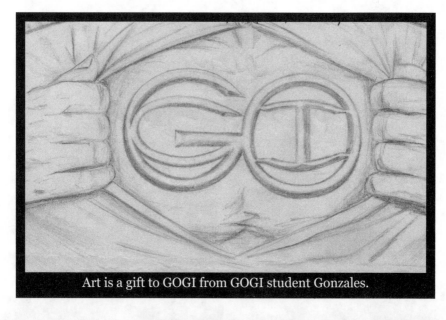

Art is a gift to GOGI from GOGI student Gonzales.

BELLY BREATHING
FEEL THE FLOW

One hand on your chest
One hand on your belly

Which hand is moving?

To use BELLY BREATHING to help you break old habits and move powerfully into a positive future, simply!

FEEL THE FLOW:
- Put one HAND ON YOUR CHEST.
- Put the other HAND ON YOUR BELLY.
- Which hand is moving?

If the hand on your chest is moving, you are not using the tool BELLY BREATHING. You are chest breathing if only your chest moves, which is the least effective and most destructive form of breathing.

If the hand on your belly is moving in and out with every breath, you are BELLY BREATHING.

If that is not easy for you, try this approach: Place your feet firmly on the ground. Now, while focusing on your feet, imagine that as you breathe, your job is to get the air all the way to your feet. Try that each day for a few minutes. It really helps.

While BELLY BREATHING sounds simple, nothing is more powerful than taking charge of how your body uses its oxygen.

♥~ *Coach Taylor*

Art is a gift to GOGI from GOGI student Lund.

Art is a gift to GOGI from GOGI student Sanchez.

—————— Chapter 6 ——————
The GOGI Tool
FIVE SECOND LIGHTSWITCH

FIVE SECOND LIGHTSWITCH is part of the set of Tools called TOOLS OF THE BODY and was created when a group of GOGI students wanted to find a way to get their actions to not be so reactive or automatic. Wanting to find a way to simply stop decisions and choices that were lightning fast and seemed out of control, they created the ability to FLIP THE SWITCH and redirect any thought within five seconds to a positive action. When you have a positive action already picked out, it is easier to FLIP THE SWITCH.

When you have your FIVE SECOND LIGHTSWITCH ready, you can make sure you don't make the same mistakes of the past. FLIP THE SWITCH and you can shine the light where you are directing your life and go that direction with confidence.

Stopping a negative thought or stopping an urge sometimes feels impossible. FIVE SECOND LIGHTSWITCH is a great Tool to help overcome this obstacle.

FIVE SECOND LIGHTSWITCH works like this: when you get consumed with "that" thought, instead of trying to get the thought to stop, simply flip your FIVE SECOND LIGHTSWITCH and replace that old thought with your new action. FIVE SECOND LIGHTSWITCH allows you to notice the thought, but not act on it. With the GOGI Tool FIVE SECOND LIGHTSWITCH, you swap the thought to a positive action within five seconds.

Count the Kids

Coach Teri is a GOGI girl who lived in the module called "GOGI Campus" at the Los Angeles County Jail. When she learned FIVE SECOND LIGHTSWITCH, she modified it to work for her. She said when she got a negative thought that entered her mind, she noticed the thought. She realized that the old thought was no longer of service to her. She then replaced that thought doing her version of FIVE SECOND LIGHTSWITCH. She holds up her hand and names her children and grandchildren on her fingers. Counting her children and grandchildren is her new positive action. She gets to the action of counting her children and grandchildren. This gives her five seconds to swap the unproductive thought with a positive action.

When you are told, "Just don't think about smoking a cigarette," it seems as if all you can think about is a cigarette. The human mind does not work well with negatives. It seems as if our mind will go to the "do not" as quickly as if you said "go for it."

As you train your mind to create positive thoughts and actions, it is nearly impossible to think that you could simply stop thinking about something which consumed a lot of thinking for so long. That is why FIVE SECOND LIGHTSWITCH works; it realizes that your mind has been trained to head down a particular road almost like its on autopilot. FIVE SECOND LIGHTSWITCH permits you to consider the old thought and then replace that thought with a new, more positive and productive action.

The Key is Yours

FIVE SECOND LIGHTSWITCH is widely considered the best of the Tools by our most impulsive GOGI students and those who claim that sometimes things happen before they realize they had the thought. The key is to have your replacement action ready.

The Tool FIVE SECOND LIGHTSWITCH was named in the gym/chapel at the U.S. Federal prison at Terminal

Island in California when a "program" format was offered to attempt to describe the brain's neural pathways to a group of inmates.

To illustrate that their actions were controllable, the group used the overhead lights in the chapel as an example. Discussions of turning on the lights which were desired and leaving the undesired lights turned off helped get the point across well.

You can think of your brain like a series of overhead lights. You get to choose which thoughts you switch on and which ones you ignore. No one is the boss of what goes on in your brain, except you. This tool can help you build new neural pathways and shine the light in the direction you want to go.

The more you associate any light going on or off as FLIP THE SWITCH, the easier it will be for you to FLIP THE SWITCH in your own mind and use your FIVE SECOND LIGHTSWITCH.

Light switches go on and off all day, every day. So, too, can your FIVE SECOND LIGHTSWITCH.

Art is a gift to GOGI from GOGI student Borjas.

FIVE SECOND LIGHTSWITCH

- STATEMENT OF OWNERSHIP -

I CAN FLIP MY 5-SECOND LIGHTSWITCH AND INSTANTLY CHANGE ANY NEGATIVE THOUGHT TO A POSITIVE ACTION. THERE IS NO NEGATIVE THOUGHT MORE POWERFUL THAN MY POSITIVE ACTION WHEN I FLIP MY 5-SECOND LIGHTSWITCH.

NEW ACTION ON

OFF OLD THOUGHT

G.O.G.I.

G.O.G.I.

- KEY WORDS -

OLD THOUGHT = NEW ACTI

I HAVE AN OLD THOUGHT AND I HAVE A NEW ACTION

My signature

Print your name   ERIC PAIT

It was not so easy at first for me, but Now with GOGI I can see the light at the end of the tunnel!

My signature _____

Print your name _____   JUON A. Chiroga

FIVE SECOND LIGHTSWITCH

I CAN FLIP THE SWITCH
OLD THOUGHT ⟶ NEW ACTION

*I have an OLD THOUGHT and,
I have a NEW ACTION*

FIVE SECOND LIGHTSWITCH is a popular tool for individuals who are impulsive or quick to act without considering the consequences. It's also a favorite tool for individuals who suffer from addiction. It is a great all-around tool for every day, too. Here's how it works:

• First, you will NOTICE the thought. Just notice it. You might think, "Wow, that old thought again?" That is OK. Just noticing is a major accomplishment for someone on autopilot.

• Once you notice the old thought, you can FLIP THE SWITCH and get to your NEW ACTION within 5 seconds. When you get to your NEW ACTION within 5 seconds, you are driving out potential for the old thought to have power over you.

With FIVE SECOND LIGHTSWITCH, you can FLIP THE SWITCH and direct your life in the direction YOU want.

Art is a gift to GOGI from GOGI student Scribblez.

———————— Chapter 7 ————————

Tools of Choice

POSITIVE THOUGHTS
POSITIVE WORDS
POSITIVE ACTIONS

The second set of GOGI Tools are designed to permit you to make positive choices in three specific areas: your thoughts, your words and your actions, and by using GOGI TOOLS OF CHOICE, you will notice your interactions with others will improve almost immediately.

The TOOLS OF CHOICE are about creating positive choices. With TOOLS OF CHOICE, you have the opportunity to show the world who you are becoming through your new, more positive choices. These GOGI Tools help you redefine yourself and help you maximize the opportunities you wish to attract.

Choose you Focus

With POSITIVE THOUGHTS, you choose to focus on the positive rather than to dwell on the negative. With POSITIVE WORDS, you choose to strengthen the world around you with your choice of words. With POSITIVE ACTIONS you choose to show the world who you are choosing to become.

Choice puts you in a place of personal control and power. You get to create a positive version of how the world gets to see you when you apply TOOLS OF CHOICE.

The GOGI Toolbox was added with these Tools when the women at the Los Angeles County Jail, who participated in the GOGI Campus program, believed they were an essential addition to their long-term change.

The "GOGI Campus" was precedent-setting for its time. Los Angeles County Sheriff's Department cleared the path for GOGI to provide programming to an exclusive housing unit that was called GOGI Campus. Female inmates were referred to as "students," and the dreary block walls were slathered with inspirational GOGI posters and art created by the more than 300 women who were admitted to the campus over a two-year period.

GOGI Girls Develop GOGI Tools

When GOGI Campus first opened, the GOGI Tools were only six in number and developed by men in a Federal prison where I had been volunteering. The women in GOGI Campus, which was a pre-sentencing jail, had a far more intense environment, and they chose to become fully immersed in GOGI. A full seven days a week, from before dawn to long after dusk, the GOGI Girls would sit in Peer Mentor Circles in the dayroom, creating GOGI classes based on Tools and subjects of importance to them.

From this daily dive into the depths of newly discovered competencies came six more Tools that completed the GOGI Toolbox. The TOOLS OF CHOICE were a gift offered by the women of GOGI Campus. One woman put it this way, "Coach Taylor, we are 24 women in this tiny, smelly, dimly-lit dungeon. We need these Tools added to our GOGI Toolbox or we will go insane."

Undecided Futures

The pre-sentencing stage of incarceration is particularly stressful, due to the uncertainty. For example, if a mother were to be sentenced for four years in prison and she did not have a suitable family member to care for the children it was likely she would lose her children to adoption. The state would provide foster care, but within two years, begin to look for a suitable long-term home for the children displaced by their parent's actions.

For one young girl who followed her gangster

boyfriend around like a lovesick puppy, when her boyfriend pulled out a gun from beneath his car seat and killed a rival gang member, it meant a prison number as his willing accomplice to the murder.

For another GOGI girl, the terror came with the agonizing realization of her drug-induced actions while running amok on the streets. In the GOGI Campus she detoxed from heroin, and her nightly tremors and wailing was heard through the thick block walls, impacting the entire Campus. As she cleared from the haze of it all, she began having nightmares of selling her own child for sex in exchange for drugs. Her wailing became inconsolable as she realized her nightmare had actually been a reality.

There were three hundred stories, three hundred broken hearts, and three hundred women determined to not give up. Day after day, 24 GOGI Girls emerged from their cells, stated their GOGI Pledge of Service to Community, then sat in their dayroom seats and studied, developed, practiced, discussed, and lived "The GOGI Way". Girls left, and new girls joined the campus, each crying crocodile tears over the events that got them there. And, each contributed in their own unique way to the development of the GOGI Culture, which offers a solution to problems and direct routes to new possibilities.

The Birthplace of the 3P's

GOGI Campus was the birthplace of the TOOLS OF CHOICE, and the 3P's within POSITIVE THOUGHTS, POSITIVE WORDS, and POSITIVE ACTIONS.

The women discovered when they filtered everything through their TOOLS OF CHOICE, they made better choices. Before a thought, word, or action, they considered: Is it Powerful? Is it Productive? Is it Positive?

Keeping Drama to a Minimum

The TOOLS OF CHOICE helped reduce the inherent angst of jail life and permitted the GOGI Girls the ability to form the habit of using these GOGI Tools daily. But, while the women of GOGI Campus were actively engaging in developing the lifestyle that would become "The GOGI Way", they were not alone.

At the Central Training Facility (CTF) of the California Department of Corrections and Rehabilitation, under the direction of Warden Marion Spearman, GOGI was permitted to have more than 100 male prisoners assemble in a large gym every Friday night. These 100 GOGI students would gather in Peer Mentor Circles of 8-12 group members. They would study their GOGI Tools according to the GOGI Calendar of Study in a series of 15 meetings before a round of study was considered "complete."

POSITIVE WORDS was the tool being discussed on a particular day when I was present as a special guest. After a general meeting where I was asked to address the entire group, I was able to sit in on some of the discussions. When I got to Coach Johnny Howe's group, they were engrossed in an activity that captivated my attention. One of the group members stood in the center of the circle. Then, one by one, each of the group members looked their peer in the eye and stated one profoundly positive thing about them; something they had come to realize or understand over the course of their weeks together.

Strong Men Strengthen Others

It was an incredible site to see grown express respect for the deep relationships created within the Peer Mentor Circle. Men were acknowledged for their level of integrity, their insight, or care for others, and willingness to become a solution rather than a burden to society.

I watched as a tear found its way down one man's cheek before he reveled through his broken voice that he could not remember hearing anything positive about himself – ever. I fought back my own tears as each man expressed gently chosen POSITIVE WORDS, which were formed from their POSITIVE THOUGHTS, and delivered in a setting of POSITIVE ACTIONS.

At that moment, while seated in Coach Johnny's Peer Mentor Circle, I realized that GOGI and "Living the GOGI Way" was much bigger than just my willingness to listen to an unheard population.

GOGI was actually enabling these men to cut directly to the core of the human purpose of finding freedom through living a life of service. This enabled them to bypass all politics and cultural limitations inherent in the setting of prison life.

A United Force for Good

The men of CTF and the GOGI Girls of GOGI Campus at a county jail were on the same journey; they were identifying simple ways to ameliorate the angst of poor decisions, and replacing a negative culture with a positive alternative they could call their own.

What the women offered as an essential addition to the GOGI Toolbox, ultimately freed the men from the confines of cultural limitations and negative norms. Through POSITIVE THOUGHTS, POSITIVE WORDS and POSITIVE ACTIONS, these men could show up in their own communities as a solution rather than an ongoing problem. While separated by block walls and many miles, these two groups of individuals were united in their dedication, and GOGI provided a solid vehicle with which they could collaborate on creating a solution for all mankind.

Accept that
Change is
Just around
the
Corner...

Go GOGI-4-Life!
Peer Coach
Penelope Fenstermaker

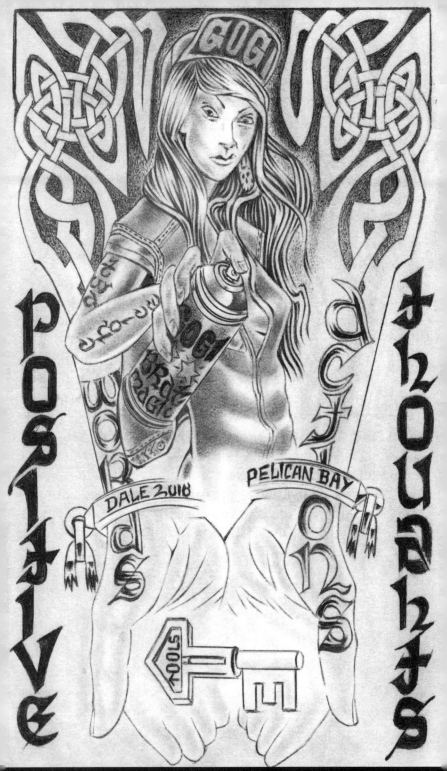

Art is a gift to GOGI from GOGI leader Dale Bretches.

—————— Chapter 8 ——————

The GOGI Tool
POSITIVE THOUGHTS

POSITIVE THOUGHTS is part of the set of Tools called TOOLS OF CHOICE and was created when a group of GOGI Girls were in a small housing module day in and day out with very little ability to get away from each other for much needed alone time. Being in a situation where alone time was not possible, this Tool was created to build their ability to withstand all sorts of peer pressure, bad attitudes, drug and alcohol addiction, and general negativity. Being in a very difficult situation, they decided that rather than to give up and give in, they would become even more committed to living positive lives. You can do this, too, with POSITIVE THOUGHTS. When negativity creeps into your head, you can banish it forever with your fix-it Tool called POSITIVE THOUGHTS.

Here is a fact: Only you can choose your thoughts. No one else can tell you what to think. You can choose to think of something positive or you can choose to think of something negative. It's simply not possible for someone else to force you to think in a certain way.

You have Choices

At any moment, you can think of a mountain, think of a song, think of a television show. Try it. Change your thoughts. Your thoughts are yours to pick, regardless of what is going on around you. You can pick any thought at any time.

And, here's another fact. Your thoughts are more powerful than you may realize. When you think of positive

things, then you will see other things in your world that are
positive. When you see the world more positively, you will
tend to experience the more positive version of the world
as well. With this tool, you will begin to "see" more positive
around you.

Turn it Around

If you sometimes feel depressed, hopeless, or
irritable, POSITIVE THOUGHTS can turn things around
quickly. This is because POSITIVE THOUGHTS is a great
Tool to use to turn the tide on your thinking, which often
times turns the tide of events in your life.

The challenge for some people in altering their
perspective is that when they are being negative, they claim
they are simply being realistic. They are so stuck on being
"right" or "honest," or dealing "truthfully" with "reality,"
that they are seeing only the negative and are stuck on how
"right" they are about something negative.

This poses a problem for them because they wallow
in negativity, committed to their "rightness." This locks
them into the negative and they become part of the problem,
not part of the solution.

"Right" is a Perspective

Until that person is willing or able to consider that
their version of "right" is just a perspective held by their
opinionated observation, there is little room for change.

POSITIVE THOUGHTS is the critical tool for
negative individuals, but unfortunately it is often positive
people who use the tool. Negative people just continue to be
negative, claiming they would be positive if things weren't
so negative.

For the GOGI Tool POSITIVE THOUGHTS to work
for the negative individual, there needs to be enough room
in their own mind to consider that being negative is one
perspective. The negative is not necessarily 100 percent
reality; nor is the negative thought the sum total of the
possibilities.

Not the Only Thought

When a negative thought enters our minds, that is not the only thought we can have. We can create many other thoughts and many other perspectives such as: "It has been worse." "It will get better." "Someone, somewhere on earth has it worse." "I can get through this tough time." "No one can make my mind negative," and an unlimited list of others.

POSITIVE THOUGHTS is a Tool we use because we may not always be positively supported by our environment. Environmentally-supported positive thoughts are easy, and often quite temporary. When we are truly owning our life experience, we create POSITIVE THOUGHTS, even in the most negative of environments.

POSITIVE THOUGHTS

IS IT POWERFUL?
IS IT PRODUCTIVE?
IS IT POSITIVE?

*With every thought,
I ask myself the three P's.*

POSITIVE THOUGHTS are yours to create. Here is how you can master POSITIVE THOUGHTS:

- NOTICE – I notice my thoughts. I created this thought.

- CONSIDER– Is my thought negative or positive? Is it helping me be positive?

- CHOICE – I have positive things I can choose to think about right now.

- SWAP – I replace all negative thoughts with something positive.

No one can intrude your mind, unless you give them permission. Every thought you have is only yours to choose. In truth, your thoughts are of your own creation. At any moment, you can think of something positive or think negative.

♥~ Coach Taylor

Art is a gift to GOGI from GOGI student Jefferies.

———————— Chapter 9 ————————

The GOGI Tool
POSITIVE WORDS

POSITIVE WORDS is part of the set of Tools called TOOLS OF CHOICE and was created by the GOGI Girls of 2008 when they realized that it was not enough to simply use POSITIVE THOUGHTS. They quickly realized that if their thoughts remained in their head, they were vulnerable to outside influence. When they used their POSITIVE WORDS, it was almost as if they were building an additional shield of protection to keep them from being negatively impacted, regardless of the outside circumstances. When they used POSITIVE WORDS, they were less inclined to become the victim of negative circumstances. You can use your words as your biggest weapon to fend off attackers of your peace of mind and positive life.

It is amazing how much you reveal about yourself when you choose your words. If you wrote down all the words you say each day, are they mostly negative or mostly positive? Do you think that others force you to choose a certain set of words? Do you make excuses for the negative words you choose?

Words contain the power to create opportunity or obstacles. With a compliment, you can change someone's day. With a criticism, you can destroy someone's hope.

You have Options

In addition to choosing to speak using the Tool POSITIVE WORDS, it is your option to associate with others who use this Tool POSITIVE WORDS. When you associate with other positively speaking individuals, you are associating with individuals who are in control of their lives. They are in a position of power; they can make the choice to focus on the positive.

Individuals who are frequently complaining, criticizing, or talking negatively about their lives or others, may find that the Tool POSITIVE WORDS will help them. This is because complaining just enhances and encourages more negativity. POSITIVE WORDS, however, helps you move beyond the negative.

Change Everything

For individuals who are prone to seeing or experiencing negativity, POSITIVE WORDS is a great Tool to change just about everything.

First off, know that your word choice is more revealing about you than you might think. The words you choose and how you say them almost always help determine what happens in your work, your home, your love, and your friendships. POSITIVE WORDS is your Tool to improve all those areas of your life, but they come at a price.

To use POSITIVE WORDS correctly, you will need to give up and LET GO of many of the words which you have heard, thought, and said for many years. You will need to LET GO of negative comments about the system, your cellie/bunkie, the cops, your spouse, your kids, your job, your boss, your life, your choices, and your history.

An Easy Filter

Here is an easy filter. Before you say a word, ask yourself, "Does what I am about to say create the opportunity for things to improve?." Don't fool yourself in thinking that tearing someone or something down has ever made things better. When dealing with humans, more is accomplished and less hurt is caused when the focus is on strengths.

Nothing good has ever come from ripping a person to shreds and expecting them to put themselves back in a better condition. That is the example we have learned from prison systems: a system which is prone to tear down the individual, punish them and expect them to be better for it.

No Better than your Words

If you are talking negatively about any human, then you are no better than the system you believe is so destructive.

Until you can learn that lifting up is more powerful than ripping apart, you are no better than those who demean and disrespect you. Here is another tough pill to swallow; it is likely you will need to change first, while still under the oppression of the criticism and condemnation of others.

Do not waste your time waiting for them to use the Tool POSITIVE WORDS. You must first make the choice to get out of the system of negativity and destruction by committing to lift up others while you are lifting up yourself in the process.

Art is a gift to GOGI from GOGI student Simpson.

With just one step at a time. Allow's
a second for ~~negative~~ Negitive thoughts to be left
behind. for, forward is the "one way" to a straight
path. fa, l. "shamis" has just begin this "program"
with just a Chance, for l could change "forever"!?
So, may l have found inner peace with in
myself at last . . . .

"l appreeciate being apart of your
program. God willing l may be
a Coach someday?"

POSITIVE WORDS

IS IT POWERFUL?
IS IT PRODUCTIVE?
IS IT POSITIVE?

*With every word I choose to speak,
I ask myself the three P's.*

POSITIVE WORDS are your tool for changing the way you see and experience your world. Here is how to use POSITIVE WORDS:

- LISTEN – I listen to what is being said.

- CONSIDER – Is my opinion positive or negative?

- GET AWAY – What good can possibly come out of this? (If there is no possibility of good I get myself or my thoughts away from the situation.)

- CHOOSE – I have selected my POSITIVE WORDS and I will choose those words right now.

- CLAIM – I am my POSITIVE WORDS. I state my POSITIVE WORDS out loud, in a letter, or as I am thinking.

Most people use the same words as they did yesterday. How can you expect things to be different when you are using the same words to communicate? The tool POSITIVE WORDS changes the course of your life from accepting how things were to creating them how you want them to be.

♥~ *Coach Taylor*

Art is a gift to GOGI from GOGI student Nicholas Marinelli.

———————— Chapter 10 ————————

The GOGI Tool
POSITIVE ACTIONS

POSITIVE ACTIONS is part of the set of Tools called TOOLS OF CHOICE. This Tool was the obvious Tool emerging from the other TOOLS OF CHOICE. This is because the GOGI Girls realized that it was possible to shield yourself from negativity by using POSITIVE THOUGHTS, and they would increase their protection by using POSITIVE WORDS, and when they used POSITIVE ACTIONS, they drove away people, places, and things that did not positively support what they wanted in life.

With practice, you can use POSITIVE ACTIONS to prove to yourself and others that it IS possible to change the course of your life and be happy, positive, sober/sane, and successful.

Using the Tool POSITIVE ACTIONS is your proof to the world that you are moving in a powerful and positive direction in your life. What you choose to read, what you choose to do with your free time and what you choose to watch are exactly that: choices. But, you also choose how you react to what happens around you.

Your reaction to disappointments and how you handle bad news tells the world who you are. POSITIVE ACTIONS is a tool to help you give the most positive response to life's inevitable challenges.

POSITIVE ACTIONS is a powerful Tool that you can use to influence others in a positive way, as well. When you choose to use the Tool POSITIVE ACTIONS, it is likely you will be making it possible for someone else to see an example of something positive.

Most individuals follow the leader; they do what they have seen done. If you make it a habit to use POSITIVE ACTIONS, you will be improving the lives of others, even if you don't immediately see the outcome.

You Lead your Life

The Tool POSITIVE ACTIONS puts you in a leadership position of your life, a respected position of an individual who possesses self-control and maturity. Using this Tool is a display of your bigger vision of life and shows that you are aware that challenges will come and you are defined by your reactions to those challenges. If you want to display the best part of you to the world, POSITIVE ACTIONS is the Tool to use.

If you are using the Tools of POSITIVE THOUGHTS and POSITIVE WORDS, then POSITIVE ACTIONS will come pretty easily. You cannot use POSITIVE THOUGHTS and POSITIVE WORDS and then not have POSITIVE ACTIONS as a natural outcome.

Even if you are struggling with negative thoughts and can't seem to get beyond negative words, the Tool POSITIVE ACTIONS will empower you to overcome the negative.

Actions are your Proof

Your use of POSITIVE ACTIONS is your proof. And, when repeated over and over again, this Tool, POSITIVE ACTIONS, can help define the new version of who you are creating yourself to be. It is not enough to do something positive one time. It is in the repetition that change becomes lasting.

Just like a professional star athlete, you must practice until success becomes a habit, change is formed, and the new definition of you emerges through repetition.

You may not want to start school because it will take 2, or 4, or 7, or 10 years to finish. You may think you can't do it, that your brain is fried, that you are too old or never really learned quickly. All that negativity can keep you from using your Tool POSITIVE ACTIONS.

One Day at a Time

It is far better to take one day at a time. Just practice one day using your tool POSITIVE ACTIONS. Just fill out the application. Just get on the list for class. Just attend church. Just go to the AA meeting. Just read that book. Just have that positive conversation. One action at a time. You create a better version of you.

When we take our head out of the clouds to bring the current moment into focus, we find that our life is built on moment-to-moment decisions. Your use of POSITIVE ACTIONS may seem like a drop of water in an ocean, but with enough drops placed in the ocean day after day, change eventually occurs.

Just accept that one drop as one precious drop of freedom. Then, create another drop, and then another.

Art is a gift to GOGI from GOGI student Christopher Oerding.

Two art pieces donated to GOGI from Coach D. Baca's art collection.

POSITIVE ACTIONS

IS IT POWERFUL?
IS IT PRODUCTIVE?
IS IT POSITIVE?

*With every action,
I ask myself the three P's.*

With the Tool POSITIVE ACTIONS, you make a declaration of where you are headed. To use POSITIVE ACTIONS all you need to do is:

- CONSIDER MY ACTION – I consider this action.
  Is it positive or does it represent my old way of being?

- PICK MY POSITIVES – I pick my positive actions.
  I have three positive actions ready and waiting.

- I CHOOSE – I am going to choose a positive action
  and leave the negative in the dust.

Things don't need to change in order for you to use your Tool POSITIVE ACTIONS. The use of this tool each day adds up and creates a solid foundation for lasting change. One BIG action is cool, but the REAL change is in the small choices you make minute by minute.   ♥~ *Coach Taylor*

Do not wrong or hate your
neighbor; for it is not
he that you wrong;
you wrong yourself.
(Positive Words)

— Native saying

It is a truth, a melancholy
truth, that the good things
which men do are often
buried in the ground, whi-
their evil dee- ds are strip-
ped naked and exposed
to the wor- ld.
(Reality Check)
(Let Go)

— Black Thunder, Fo,

Kasindini Sanikua R. Ojeda
— Semi Mature Golden Eagle Feather —

—————— Chapter 11 ——————
Tools of Moving Forward

CLAIM RESPONSIBILITY
LET GO
FOR–GIVE

The next section of Tools are The TOOLS OF MOVING FORWARD. For some individuals, these Tools are the most challenging because they require introspection and insight. Some individuals would rather have things remain the same and complain about them because it is easier that way.

The TOOLS OF MOVING FORWARD require that you be willing to move forward, leaving things that may be getting in the way of your progress and internal happiness.

You can Move Forward

The TOOLS OF MOVING FORWARD are about moving forward in your life. TOOLS OF MOVING FORWARD help you with moving beyond the past. Unless you are prepared to use the Tools, CLAIM RESPONSIBILITY, LET GO, and FOR–GIVE, there is little room for lasting change.

When you use the Tool CLAIM RESPONSIBILITY for your actions and reactions, along with the Tools LET GO for daily irritants and FOR–GIVE, to get distance from harm, there is room in your head, your heart, and your soul for positive decision-making. By the time we are thirteen years old, we benefit if we are able to move forward and not languish in the swelling number of bad things we have witnessed or endured in our short stay on earth. The problem is, moving beyond bad things is not a subject taught in schools. Parents are often ignorant or are actually the cause of the bad things, so looking toward them for the teaching might not be productive.

Moving Past the Past

The set of Tools GOGI created to deal with these inevitable life challenges are called the TOOLS OF MOVING FORWARD. These Tools enable us to create the present and a future unencumbered by the negative aspects of all we have endured.

While most of us never learn these Tools when we most needed them in our teens, it is never too late to apply them. And, in doing so, the pain of our teenage years seems to melt away with little resistance.

In my observation of individuals in prison, it seems to hold true that life starts to unravel in outwardly noticeable ways as we hit our teenage years, often creating a spiral from which few emerge unscathed.

The pain we suffered earlier in our lives often begins to be revealed in our decisions, our choice of friends, and our behavior. We act out, sometimes not even truly realizing why.

We may show signs of low self esteem, insecurity, anxiety, depression, rage, or a wide variety of behaviors, permitting our elders to start slapping labels or medications on us.

The TOOLS OF MOVING FORWARD promote the early dumping of as much baggage as possible, as frequently as possible, with less suffering as one takes on more of life's responsibilities.

CLAIM RESPONSIBILITY

CLAIM RESPONSIBILITY gives you the power to move beyond decisions of the past and be totally and completely focused on today's decisions which are most important. This is powerful because we often link the bad decisions of the past to the present and get stuck in the loop of harm, repeating the same bad decisions and naively hoping for a different outcome. Isolating each decision when we use this Tool helps us keep things new, fresh and less likely to be tainted by the past.

LET GO

With the handy Tool LET GO, you can simply do a quick HAND/SQUASH/TOSS of any emotion that stands in your way of happiness, thereby moving forward beyond the temptation to circle back to reengage with people, places or things that have rattled your cage. You won't really be "letting go" of anything when you use this tool. You simply get it out of your way so you can move beyond its tendency to stop your progress.

FOR-GIVE

And, lastly the Tool FOR-GIVE helps you find safety from harm so you can move forward with creating an awesome life.

Are you Defined By Suffering?

In my own life, The TOOLS OF MOVING FORWARD were possibly the most difficult set of tools to master. This is because my life suffering was excusable without these Tools. For as long as I could blame others for my circumstance, I did not need to use the Tool CLAIM RESPONSIBILITY for my present life experience. For as long as I held tight to all the pain I suffered, I did not need to use the Tool LET GO to free myself from continual angst. For as long as I hovered around pain-causing people, places and things, I could not use the safety Tool of FOR-GIVE so I could not think beyond my own petty needs.

By ignoring the TOOLS OF MOVING FORWARD, I had every reason to complain and suffer. This was very convenient and, in fact, very familiar. I was, as a result of my suffering, actually defined in a way that was oddly comfortable. I worked really diligently to not be the victim, but in continuing to recant all the injustices of my life, I just kept working in circles, never really moving forward.

For me, change did not occur overnight. In fact, my changes were so subtle that they went unnoticed by everyone, even me. Through my practice of the Tools each and every waking moment, I realized a few thoughts here and there were different. I got an inkling that maybe, just maybe, I could begin to ignore the injustices and not carry them with me to my grave.

Slow Growth is Lasting

I began to CLAIM RESPONSIBILITY for what was going on in the moment, unhooking them from past events that would normally make it convenient to claim as not in my control. Then, ever so subtly, I would HAND/SQUASH/TOSS away things that were daily irritants, using LET GO to make more space in my mind to focus on those things that were working well in my life.

The kicker was when it came to FOR-GIVE, because this is the "safety" Tool. This Tool requires us to get a safe distance from harm. For me, I needed distance from otherwise close relations whenever I felt heightened emotions or expectations of something different than what was delivered.

If my emotions were high around someone else's words, actions, or lack thereof, I simply needed a "safe" distance from them until I could better manage my reactions and responses. Realizing it was unlikely that they would change, and coming to terms with the fact that they were genetically linked to me and not likely to be absent from my life forever, I needed to get "safe" enough from the harm I was causing myself in expecting something different than what they were willing or able to deliver. FOR-GIVE helped me get the distance I needed to develop the skills I needed to not to let "them" control my life's outcome.

A Frightening Question

I came to the point where defining myself as my past

was no longer relevant to the life I wanted to create. Who was I, really, if I was not my suffering? Who was I if I was not defined by my past? These are frightening questions when asked with deep intention to reveal the truth. I discovered it's far more convenient to remain a victim, yet, I was too weary to play out the next 50 years in the same manner.

Not Playing to your Weaknesses

The TOOLS OF MOVING FORWARD are not for the weak, but they are for the weary. For the individual who is simply tired of being tired, the TOOLS OF MOVING FORWARD are a welcome reprieve. It takes every bit of remaining strength to make the decision to leave the baggage behind and take that step into the unknown, realizing – at long last – that even the unknown has to be better than one more round of the past.

Emotional Prisons

The personal prison I experienced in my life was an emotional prison created by my lack of coping tools to enable me to move forward. I was stuck in the loop of harm and the more I languished there, the deeper the hole got, and the more impossible it was for me to get myself out. My inability to move forward was the root cause for my mental prison.

The women of GOGI Campus would concur that a majority of their addiction and poor decisions as adults were a result of not being able to move beyond abuses or violations of their childhood. A full 80 percent of the women in the jail module called GOGI Campus reported sexual abuse as a child. Most witnessed violence. Nearly all stated they experienced trauma. They were unable to move beyond experiences and felt doomed to repeat cycles of poor decisions.

Moving Beyond Trauma

Girls are not the only victims of traumatic

Art is a gift to GOGI from GOGI student Rey.

childhoods. Boys are molested, beaten, and abused far more frequently than is documented. These boys end up addicted to drugs or acting out in an effort to move beyond the trauma. Their shame is often funneled into choices that may impede their ability to move forward. Acting on all they have available to them, poor choices are the only means with which they find solace. A prison term as an adult is the likely outcome for these boys who suffer at a level of silence that few understand.

Who Am I?

Let me share with you a story, one of millions that make up the experiences of far too many children. We will call him R, but his real name is chiseled into my mind. He was the first prisoner who shared the horrors of his childhood with me as he waged a desperate attempt to reconcile his life using GOGI Tools. I never met R, except through his letters to the GOGI mail room. When he began his study of the TOOLS OF MOVING FORWARD, he nearly halted and terminated any future study.

His biggest concern, his letter stated, was how he would define himself if not by his past. Who was R if he was not the young boy who was locked in the dog cage outside the rundown trailer called home? Who was R if he was not the boy sold for sexual favors by his drunkard stepfather who would sit and drink while R was being raped in the bedroom nearby? Who was R if he was not the man sentenced to a life in prison for murder?

We may find that defining ourselves by our past experience is a logical method of figuring out what is likely to be the present and future. History is generally the best predictor of future events, unless there is a concerted effort to move beyond previous limits and create a new opportunity.

When what we have experienced in the past simply will not work for the ever-so faint vision of the future, that is when the TOOLS OF MOVING FORWARD come in very handy.

--------- Chapter 12 ---------

The GOGI Tool
CLAIM RESPONSIBILITY

CLAIM RESPONSIBILITY is part of the set of Tools called TOOLS OF MOVING FORWARD. This Tool is not about claiming responsibility for the past. Instead, the Tool CLAIM RESPONSIBILITY is about today and tomorrow. When you use this Tool, you realize that how you respond and react to anything is under your direct command. No one can make you angry. It is you who gets to choose if you will let others anger you. No one can make you violent. It is you who gets to choose if you will let others bring out violence in your behavior. No one can make you drink or use drugs. It is you who gets to choose if you put yourself in a position where saying no is a challenge. When you use CLAIM RESPONSIBILITY, you move forward toward a life you may have never thought possible.

There are many ways to interpret the words "Claim" and "Responsibility." Together, the way GOGI uses these words as a Tool, they provide a powerful way to gain perspective with which you can move forward in your life. There are many things that happened to and around you in the past, many of them were your responsibility and many things were not your responsibility, or you had no knowledge or choice in the matter. Using CLAIM RESPONSIBILITY as a GOGI Tool is not about the past at all.

GOGI does not focus on reconciling the past because it could take years, and possibly a lifetime, to understand what occurred and why, and to unravel the mess that resulted. GOGI is about creating a positive future for individuals trying to resolve the past. The fact is, the past is more easily reconciled when you have momentum moving positively into the present and future.

Your Choices

Rather than remain stuck and unable to move forward, CLAIM RESPONSIBILITY as a Tool is about your choices today. It is kind of like having a broken car at the side of the road, but not having any tools or help to fix it. You can remain at the side of the road all day long complaining about how you have a broken car, or you can gather up the things you need, shut the car door, and start walking toward your freedom.

Today is Yours

The students of GOGI don't want you to remain stuck in the past forever, reliving what you did or what happened. That actually creates a vacuum and disables any insight you might gain from the past. CLAIM RESPONSIBILITY as a tool states that no matter what happened or what you did in the past, today is yours to become part of the solution and make positive decisions.

With CLAIM RESPONSIBILITY, you have power over your actions and your reactions today and forevermore. It does not diminish your actions of the past, or permit you to remain stuck in them. Getting unstuck is the key to developing insight.

When you use CLAIM RESPONSIBILITY, how you act and how you react is no longer tied to a terrible childhood, an addiction, a criminal background, a gang membership, not having a father, drinking too much, a greedy mentality, a death, a betrayal, abuse, or anything else which might have provoked you to do things you regret.

Gaining Forward Momentum

If you are an individual with a lot of history and a heavy weight of the past slowing your ability to move forward, CLAIM RESPONSIBILITY permits you to gain forward momentum. Once you have forward momentum, the past is more easily reconciled, insight can be achieved, and lasting change can occur.

As a GOGI Tool, we use CLAIM RESPONSIBILITY in a slightly different manner than the words suggest. Remember, we are using CLAIM RESPONSIBILITY as a Tool, not as something your teacher, parent or parole board want you to do. CLAIM RESPONSIBILITY is a proactive Tool and that relates to the future.

Let's clarify. You can certainly claim an appropriate level of responsibility for your deeds of the past. You can also claim an appropriate level of responsibility for your actions. That is different than using CLAIM RESPONSIBILITY as a GOGI Tool. This is because at GOGI, we are less concerned about the past and more concerned about your ability to make better choices today. We find that as a GOGI Tool, CLAIM RESPONSIBILITY promotes positive decision making in the present and future.

The Tool and the Process

That does not mean you go into a parole hearing after doing 30 years and tell them, "Well, I study GOGI and at GOGI we don't care about the past, we only use CLAIM RESPONSIBILITY as a Tool for creating a good future." We would hope you have enough perspective that you can simultaneously use your Tools for your future while claiming responsibility for your past actions.

As a Tool, you can use CLAIM RESPONSIBILITY to take charge of your actions, your reactions, your opinions, your words, and your responses to every single thing from this day forward. Your Tool CLAIM RESPONSIBILITY does not let anyone else take over your life creating process.

With CLAIM RESPONSIBILITY, everyone and everything is kept out of the decision making boardroom of your brain. Only YOU are in charge of how you react, act, perceive, and respond. With CLAIM RESPONSIBILITY as a GOGI Tool, you will never say, "He made me mad,"

"It's your fault," or "If it was not for my situation, I would be happy." That kind of thinking is just not going to work for you. It disables you and makes you a victim of circumstance.

At GOGI, we know you can be the creator of a better life, and CLAIM RESPONSIBILITY is your Tool to help you do just that.

CLAIM RESPONSIBILITY

AM I PROUD OF THIS CHOICE?

I am responsible for all my actions and all my reactions today

As a GOGI Tool, CLAIM RESPONSIBILITY is easy because it has less to do with the past and everything to do with this moment, on this day, and from now on. Here is how to use CLAIM RESPONSIBILITY:

- CONSIDER – What is happening around me?
- I AM IN CHARGE – I am in charge of my actions and reactions today.
- I OWN IT – I can choose how to respond right now. I OWN TODAY.

CLAIM RESPONSIBILITY is a great way to stop blaming others, the system, or yourself for things. It puts you in control of your life from this day forward. Ask yourself, "Am I proud of this choice?"

How you react and how you respond is 100 percent in your control when you use CLAIM RESPONSIBILITY. With this tool, today becomes yours to create as a positive step forward in your life.

♥*~ Coach Taylor*

Getting Out
by Going In

LET GO

—————— Chapter 13 ——————

The GOGI Tool
LET GO

LET GO is part of the set of Tools called TOOLS OF MOVING FORWARD and was created for people who have a tendency to carry the heavy load of their past with them into the present and the future. By putting negative thoughts about people, places and things in your hand, and giving them the HAND/SQUASH/TOSS, you will find there is more room in your head and your heart for more positive life choices. To actually be a better person, you must move forward beyond the heavy darkness intruding on your decisions today. Regret is essential, but wallowing in regret so long that it makes for other poor decisions is just not smart. Give it the HAND/SQUASH/TOSS and commit to using LET GO so you can move forward and make more positive choices.

LET GO can be a challenging Tool for many people. This is often because once something happens, something terrible or massively influential in your life, your life changes around that event. Thoughts, words, actions, and your very being adjust to what happened.

This could be that someone close to you was killed, or something really bad happened to you as a child. It could be the first time you got high, or when you were abandoned or betrayed. It could be the trauma you experienced from falling victim to an addiction which stole years of your life from you.

Whatever the negative event was, it became part of your identity, causing you to exclude choices and decisions which may have been more positive.

LET GO might sound like an easy Tool, but it is not that easy for many individuals. Here's an example which shows just how difficult it is. If you swap the situation described below to fit your own life, you will understand why the Tool LET GO seems nearly impossible for many people. Could it be that holding on to the past is the reason people play out unproductive and negative lifestyles?

Who are You?

Let's say, in this example, you have identified yourself as someone from "Your City" all your life. You are "the one" everyone comes to you for advice and counsel. Your life in "Your City" just so happens to create an environment where drugs, crime, and people getting locked up happen every day. You are important in "Your City." You have a place, a life, a reputation, and a history.

But, what happens if you move forward in your life and are not living in "Your City," and instead you move somewhere where no one knows you? What happens if you are in another town?

Here is what probably happens. Your entire identity may be changing. It's a challenge because you do not feel accepted by the people in the new town because you think, talk and act like someone who has been around drinking, drugs, jail, and violence your entire life.

It is likely you identify with the people in the new town who are similar to your past and they drink, do drugs, and talk a lot about things that are illegal.

So, What's Next?

Do you see that using the Tool LET GO may not always be easy? The LET GO Tool is not always easy, nor is it for the weak. Using LET GO for those things that create negativity in your life can seem lonely, boring, confusing, or depressing. In this case, the Tool LET GO may seem downright impossible to use successfully. People often ask, "If I use LET GO, then what will I get as a replacement?

If you no longer identify yourself as someone of

importance in "Your City," then who are you? Here is another example: if your focus is to do whatever it takes to be a drug treatment counselor for kids, then that new identity needs to be so clear in your mind that the old identity is replaced and you begin to be an example for good. Having something positive to hold on to, makes the use of LET GO easier.

Let Go in Present Time

Additionally, the GOGI Tool, LET GO, permits you to handle the present more powerfully. Use LET GO to rid yourself of the need for instant retaliation which will only get you in more trouble. Did someone disrespect you? Has someone lied, cheated, or stole? Use LET GO to replace the need for immediate revenge.

Use LET GO to keep from overreacting, reacting too quickly, creating drama, or dragging others down that old worn road which leads to trouble. The Tool LET GO keeps you from falling back into old patterns because you HAND/ SQUASH/TOSS your way into the future.

Lighten Up with LET GO

LET GO helps you move beyond all that has happened, and all the negative which is included in your definition of self. LET GO is a great Tool if you are tired of carrying the weight of negativity around throughout your life. But, it will require practice.

Practice is the only way we can perfect a skill. LET GO is a Tool, but use of the Tool can become a skill. This Tool, can still be painful for some. That is why we keep it simple. We do not want you to try to use LET GO for the big stuff too soon. After all, it is the big stuff which may have defined you for a very long time. It would be impractical to suggest you simply use LET GO for the very thing which consumed your life thus far.

A die-hard GOGI student wrote this about the Tool LET GO: "I sit here now with the last of my life story, but afraid to use LET GO because I feel maybe I will disappear."

What a profound realization he had while on his GOGI journey. When what we have experienced in our life IS our life, how CAN we use LET GO?

The Little Stuff

So, rather than feel as if you may disappear, you can use LET GO on the little stuff. Here is an example. Someone is making noises that are irritating? Rather than let it irritate you, practice LET GO. Use the Tool LET GO and rid yourself of anything which might hold you back from being or feeling your best. Is your depression causing you to swim in a sea of negativity? Use the tool LET GO and rid yourself of thoughts in which keep you in negative waters.

GOGI students tell us that the simple act of putting the negativity in the palm of their hand, squashing it, and then tossing it away, gets the emotion and the negativity out of their body so they can think more positively.

Keep It Simple

Keeping it simple is always the best way to learn a new skill. When you can put most of life's irritations in the palm of your hand, squash them, and get them out of your mind, only then will you be prepared to start tackling the big stuff.

Using the Tool LET GO could be your freedom from being the victim or creating a victim, but it is important to use the Tool LET GO to stop victimizing yourself with negativity first. Use LET GO for the little stuff and sometimes the big stuff disappears along the way. You won't personally disappear, but the negativity diminishes and the new you has room to emerge.

HAND / SQUASH / TOSS

A simple way to use LET GO when in doubt, is to put the thought that is bothering you in your hand and give it the HAND / SQUASH / TOSS. When you use LET GO, you are free to move forward.

LET GO

HAND/SQUASH/TOSS

When bothered,
I put the concern in my hand,
squash it, and toss it away from me

LET GO is challenging for some, but here is a simple way to begin to practice LET GO in your daily life so that eventually you can use the Tool to LET GO of the big stuff that causes big pain. Here is how to use LET GO every day:

- HAND – I imagine that thought or feeling in my hand, out of my mind and out of my body.

- SQUASH – I crumple up that concern, thought or feeling. I have the power to squash it.

- TOSS – I can LET GO and toss it in the trash, or the toilet, or the sky, or to the ground. I LET GO and let it go.

- LET GO – Out loud or silently I say, "I LET GO of anything and everything that holds me back."

Once you get really good at using LET GO and are ready to move beyond day-to-day irritations, you can use LET GO to help you move beyond the big stuff, too.
♥~ Coach Taylor

———————— Chapter 14 ————————

The GOGI Tool
FOR-GIVE

FOR-GIVE is part of the set of Tools called TOOLS OF MOVING FORWARD. In truth, this is the GOGI "safety" Tool. This tool gives you permission to get a safe distance from harmful people, places and things. When you are a safe distance from harm, you will naturally find yourself giving back to others. When you are under attack or in danger, you will become selfish and uncaring. As a safety Tool, FOR-GIVE has you asking what you need to do to get a safe distance from harm. In asking that question, you are putting yourself in a position to be a benefit to yourself, your family, friends and community. When you are safe from harm, you will undoubtedly begin to give back to others. FOR you to GIVE, you must be SAFE FROM HARM. Get safe, then give back with your handy tool FOR-GIVE.

FOR–GIVE as a Tool is not about forgiveness. The two are different. FOR–GIVE is a Tool, not a concept. Most religions and most cultures teach the power of forgiveness, which frees you from many negative emotions and feelings. The difference is that the GOGI Tool FOR–GIVE can help you come to a greater understanding and easier application of forgiveness in your life.

FOR–GIVE as a Tool requires that you protect yourself. This is because it is not wise to forgive someone for hitting you when they are standing in front of you with their fists raised. You would be much wiser to protect yourself first. Forgiveness is not wise when danger is at hand. If you are suffering from a meth addiction, it is not wise, or even possible, to forgive yourself while you are actively using or in the recovery process.

Before you can use the Tool FOR–GIVE, you need a huge support system, a change of peers, an alignment with an alternative culture, and all sorts of skills and Tools to move beyond the vulnerable state in which you find yourself. FOR–GIVE is a Tool you can use to remind yourself to get distance from harm.

FOR-GIVE is not Forgive

A child who suffered sexual abuse can use the Tool FOR–GIVE when they are no longer at risk for continuation of the abuse, even if this can only occur when they become an adult. An individual can also use the Tool FOR–GIVE to move beyond the actions of their past if they have truly corrected their thinking and behavior so that they are not in danger of repeating the same action.

FOR–GIVE, as a GOGI Tool, states that it is not enough to say or hear the words "I am sorry." There must be safety from further harm for the Tool FOR–GIVE to work properly.

FOR–GIVE requires distance, protection, and the positive choices which lead to freedom. This does not mean you do not feel remorse or trauma for what happened, but it does mean that you do not need to relive the past over and over again.

More than the Past

Reliving the past only creates more of the past. If you wallow in the past, your present and your future will be filled with wallowing and may result in more angst and more pain. This creates more negativity. To actually develop insight and have a meaningful life, you can move beyond any previous action and be of positive service to others, no matter what has happened in the past.

To use the GOGI Tool FOR–GIVE is as simple as asking yourself, "Am I still at risk of being hurt or hurting others?" If you are at risk, you need to protect yourself. If you are safe from harming self or others, then FOR–GIVE permits you to have a new perspective of being of service and giving back. FOR–GIVE states that no matter what has occurred in the past, it does not define who you are today.

Get Distance

No matter what you did, "they" did, what you experienced, or the harm you caused; if it is unlikely it will happen again, then you can use your tool FOR–GIVE and to move forward. FOR–GIVE can be thought of as a Tool to help you to give back, using what happened in the past as your testament to how much an individual can change. "For-me-to-give I must be safe from harm." That is the Tool FOR-GIVE.

FOR-GIVE Is An Action

Forgive is a word that is used frequently and asked of us with equal frequency. FOR–GIVE as a GOGI Tool, however, is very different from the word forgive. FOR–GIVE as a Tool is an action item. It requires action on your part and has little to do with engaging in conversation with another.

Don't misunderstand, at GOGI we know forgiving is important. And, to address hurts and harms with others, to ask for, and to give, forgiveness is the backbone of nearly every spiritual study, religion and culture.

FOR–GIVE as a Tool, however, is simply a Tool you can use to get beyond the hurt or harm caused by self or others. When you get beyond the harm, it is easier for forgiveness to emerge.

The Protection Tool

So, as a Tool, FOR–GIVE is mainly about protection. The real question in using the Tool FOR–GIVE is, "are you a sufficient distance from the harm-causing person or circumstance?" With this Tool, you look for protection from further harm, because until you are a sufficient distance from the harm, there is no point in trying to forgive.

As a Tool, FOR–GIVE requires that you get distance from the harm. Let's say your harm is a gambling habit. You can say "sorry" and "please forgive me" a million times, but if you won't or can't stop gambling, you are too close to harm. Harm is still hovering.

FOR–GIVE as a Tool requires that you do everything and anything to distance yourself from the harmful actions or the harmful person.

For you to Give

Ultimately, FOR–GIVE is your Tool FOR you to GIVE back, give to others, and get out of your small world created by the harm. When we are harmed or harm ourselves, our world begins to revolve around the harm and we lose sight of our innate need to GIVE to others. FOR us to GIVE, we must be safe enough from harm that our world gets larger and includes observing and serving the needs of others.

FOR us to GIVE, we need distance from harm. That is the critical difference between forgiveness as a spiritual concept and FOR–GIVE as a GOGI Tool.

Art is a gift to GOGI from GOGI student Willaim Granados.

FOR–GIVE

FOR-GIVE IS MY SAFETY TOOL.
For me to give
I need distance from harm.

*For me to give, I unhook from the past,
and find my internal freedom.*

FOR–GIVE is our safety Tool. FOR-GIVE is your permission to move forward and put a stop to recurring pain. In a real way, FOR–GIVE is your ticket away from the harm, even if you were the one who caused the harm. Here is how to use the GOGI Tool FOR–GIVE:

- WHAT IS THE HARM? – What hurts the most? Where in my life do I hold resentments? Where am I disappointed, in rage or angered?

- GET DISTANCE – Am I a sufficient distance from potential harm? Is there a way for me to be hurt this way again? If so, I will get away.

- <u>FOR the GIVE</u> – FOR me to GIVE, I unhook from the past and get to safety. With my new distance from the pain, I can choose to do something nice for someone else. I choose to be of service.

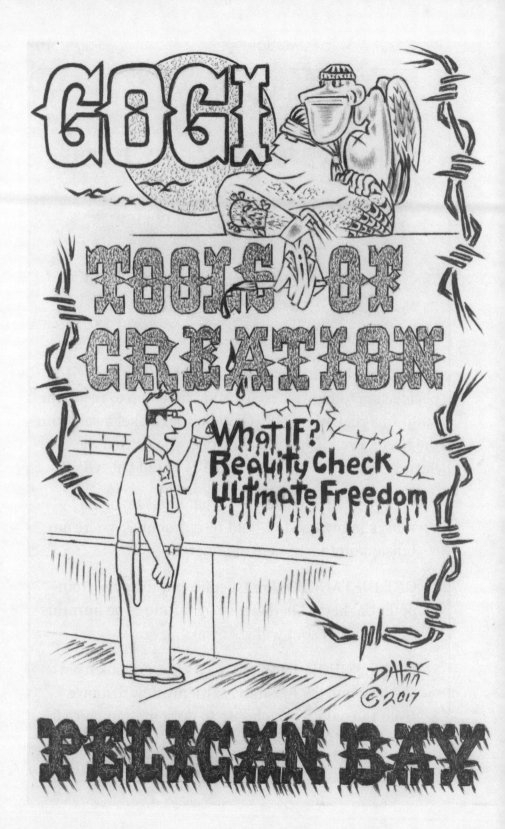

—————— Chapter 15 ——————

Tools of Creation

WHAT IF
REALITY CHECK
ULTIMATE FREEDOM

The next set of Tools we will explore are The TOOLS OF CREATION. These Tools permit you to create a positive life experience, regardless of your current mailing address.

The TOOLS OF CREATION permit you to become creative with your future. THE TOOLS OF CREATION are about how to move powerfully into the life you have always wanted, but probably did not think was possible.

You get to Dream

With your GOGI Tools, you get to dream with WHAT IF and make room for new and different possibilities. REALITY CHECK lets you come to realize you are not perfect and you are likely to make mistakes. REALITY CHECK keeps shame and hopelessness out of the change process and permits you to quickly recover from your mistakes. ULTIMATE FREEDOM is about using the most positive aspects of who you are to create a better world. Living your life in service of others is the only true and lasting freedom that does not require the convenience of things going your way. ULTIMATE FREEDOM can never be taken away and it gives back much more than the investment you make.

The set of Tools explored in the follow chapters is the set called the TOOLS OF CREATION. This set of Tools was designed to free you from the erroneous perception that things will not change, or your life is limited to current circumstance. If you diligently practice your skill level with the three Tools in this set, you will find an unlimited and unrestricted potential for your life within your grasp.

The TOOLS OF CREATION require that you be brave enough to consider your life as more than circumstantial and consider yourself as more than a victim of the situations swirling around your choices each day.

Bravery isn't Cheap

While it isn't cheap, bravery has a few requirements for sustainability. It requires an innate faith in something greater or more powerful than oneself. For some, this may be reliance upon God or faith in a divine order of things. For others, it is a mission or vision for the future that is so strong that natural fear is overshadowed. And for some, those individuals like me, bravery was the last option available as blaming others, or cursing the "system" and complaining about all I had been denied didn't seem to work very well.

Regardless of how you get to the bravery, be it divine or desperation, it will take a consistent dose of bravery before the Tools in this set even begin to make sense. And, be forewarned, there are multiple forms of bravery and only one form works in developing a sustainable freedom. There is the bravery that comes with a temporary adrenaline rush, and there is the bravery that is the slow burn, the igniting and tending to the slow burn you keep aflame even during a torrential downpour.

Bravery is Developed Daily

The good news is, and I can personally attest to this, bravery can be developed. Like most of us, I was not born automatically brave. This was an aspect of my life that I cultivated over years of determination. I have witnessed it in others, I have done it for myself, and I speak from my heart when I say that you will experience great levels of internal freedom growing ever so incrementally when you nurture the slow burn of bravery.

To do this, you will start small; pick one simple action each day that requires you to expand and grow beyond your current comfort level. This may be as simple as picking a "Positive Word of the Day" and making certain you use that word in conversations no fewer than ten times before you pull your feet up off the floor at nightfall. It may be as simple as making eye contact and offering a simple smile to a specific type of person you have previously ignored, and making certain you do this no fewer than 10 times a day. Or, it can be as simple as brushing your teeth with the opposite hand than you have dictated as your regular toothbrush holding hand.

Developing bravery is best when in small and consistent doses.

Getting your Creations Going

This set of Tools, WHAT IF, REALITY CHECK and ULTIMATE FREEDOM, are about your often-hidden powers to direct your life's outcomes. If a specifically desired outcome is not likely, you are able to create within your limitations the unrestricted experience of freedom – even in the face of what appears to be an immovable obstacle.

For example, the individual who has lost an arm may use all the GOGI Tools in the world, but the original arm is not likely to be re-attached to the body. Using the GOGI Tools, however, it is possible for this individual to develop the ability to empower other physically disabled individuals. It is possible to develop reading or video materials to help new amputees deal with the inherent challenges of losing a limb. It is possible for this individual to seek support for a robotic arm, or a prosthetic arm. There are opportunities to make a positive contribution even while experiencing limitations.

The point is, while some facts simply will not change, how you manage to create freedom beyond those facts defines your creative life expression. That is when your bravery comes into play. Luckily, within each set of GOGI Tools are the natural and simplified building blocks for bravery, enabling you to create from a place of strength, not suffer from a place of perceived victimization of self.

When taught to individuals who are actively and bravely engaged in the quest for freedom, the TOOLS OF CREATION seem to act in the same way an injection of NOS does to a race car, catapulting the individual to even greater levels of internal freedom.

WHAT IF

When GOGI Girl, Teri, rushed down the stairs from her second-tier jail cell and excitedly approached me with childlike enthusiasm, the WHAT IF tool was added to the GOGI Toolbox.

"Coach Taylor, Coach Taylor!," she exclaimed.

"Yes, Teri. What is it?" I replied.

"Coach Taylor. What if I am not my past?"

WHAT IF was added to the GOGI Toolbox that day.

It had never occurred to me that some individuals would remain stuck in defining themselves by their addiction, but that is truly the case. Addiction may cause an individual to define their life by a substance and as a result, feel helpless, hopeless, and even powerless to effect change. Addiction is like any other circumstance in which you may choose to define yourself or you may create other constructs that limit your freedom.

In my experience with those who are suffering, it seems that when an individual states they are powerless over something, they self-define as that very thing over which they feel we have no power. Saying, "I am a meth addict" is a different prospective than "I am addicted to meth." Meth addiction does not need to be the limit of their life experience.

The question Teri asked is one we all may ask ourselves with each and every decision. WHAT IF there is another possibility just around the corner that is just as valid, just as strong, just as truthful?

Teri came to the realization that while she was powerless over a specific thing presented to her in a specific way, she was entirely in control over the people, places and things related to that which she felt she had no control. Only the brave (or in my case, totally desperate) individual is inclined to question every preconceived notion. The brave, or the desperate, ask questions in an effort to break free of otherwise limiting self-definition.

Here is a real-life example. I travel often, visiting GOGI leaders and helping them expand the GOGI Culture. While on the road, I am fairly vulnerable in that my internet connections are frequently public, and shared with some individuals who have not yet been exposed to the joy of Living the GOGI Way.

I have been stolen from, lied to, and manipulated as a result of the vulnerability resulting from a lot of public contact and exposure to strangers. For a while, I believed I had no control over thieves who tap into credit cards and bank accounts to steal money. I believed it was just part of the pain and disappointment I needed to endure in making myself available to those who were limited in awareness of the joy that comes from positive life choices. With WHAT IF, however, I came to realize that I have great power over my computer passwords, and where I log onto the internet. Ultimately, I can protect credit cards, identification cards, and other documents.

In using this Tool, I realize I am not powerless over thieves, as there are specific actions I can take to reduce my vulnerability. Sure, I am powerless over thieves if I am careless, but I am no longer careless. I am no longer complacent about being violated and treated less than honorably. I am, in fact, brave when I use my WHAT IF Tool. I use my WHAT IF and I ask, "WHAT IF I avoid as much possible danger as I am able?"

I have even gotten so good at this Tool that I can now help others protect themselves as well. It is quite regular that I remind volunteers not to leave doors unlocked, do not leave purses or wallets or cash in plain view, do not leave anything visible in a car, do not leave bicycles outside even if they are locked, do not tempt anyone to live in a way that is inconsistent with enhancing the safety of others. Do not tempt the weak, expecting them to be strong. As a student of the GOGI Tools, I know I can fortify a weak situation by making strong and positive choices.

WHAT IF is about expanding beyond a limiting "reality" and defining the world from a perspective of strength. WHAT IF you are not your past? Who are you? That is the question this Tool requests you ask of yourself.

REALITY CHECK

Before it became one of the GOGI Tools, there were Tools with which to make more positive decisions, but there was a void in allowing failure and backsliding to be experienced from a place of power and learning. REALITY CHECK is the Tool used when, as we explore and expand our life experiences, we also fall short of perfection and sometimes create quite a mess of things. This tendency to fail is particularly acute with individuals suffering from addiction and a situation which played out all too often in the formative years of the GOGI Culture.

REALITY CHECK was a tool born of many tears and shattered hopes as self-proclaimed GOGI Girls were released from the GOGI Campus at the Los Angeles County Jail. They tended to be certain, convinced beyond all convincing, that armed with their GOGI Tools they would remain sober. Then, before we could celebrate their successes, I would receive word from jail staff that our very confident GOGI Girl was back in "Receiving" at the jail, arrested for yet another drug offense.

What I found when I interviewed these women, is that this failure came as a bigger blow than all prior arrests.

They were "certain" that having the GOGI Tools would have guaranteed a perfect life, free from the addiction that plagued them for many years leading up to their opportunities at the GOGI Campus.

REALITY CHECK helped each one of them realize the ten steps forward they experienced in their Campus training were not erased by the two steps back that resulted in re-arrest. No one could take away the ten steps forward and the knowledge gained in each of those steps, and only they were responsible for the two steps back. REALITY CHECK was added to the Toolbox to create something positive even amid the imperfections of human life.

ULTIMATE FREEDOM

ULTIMATE FREEDOM is a self-regeneration Tool in that the more you use it, the more it shows up in other aspects of your life. This Tool is like putting on a pair of goggles with enhanced vision capabilities that permit you to see beneath the superficial nature of daily life and into the bigger picture of all things.

When armed with ULTIMATE FREEDOM, and the perspective it enhances, you continually experience the power of purpose and meaning. This tool is all about your ability to be a creator of positivity, and your ability to bless the lives of everyone around you to see beyond "reality" into the world of possibility.

When you dedicate each and every morning to literally making the world a better place because of your positive attitude and your willingness to be helpful to others, it is only then that the end of your day can be met with complete and total satisfaction. Humans are designed as expansive creators of life; and, through the use of this Tool, we can accomplish great things that bring even greater internal freedom.

Your Creative Genius Within

The GOGI TOOLS OF CREATION may seem simple. They may even seem obvious. But, if that is the case, why do

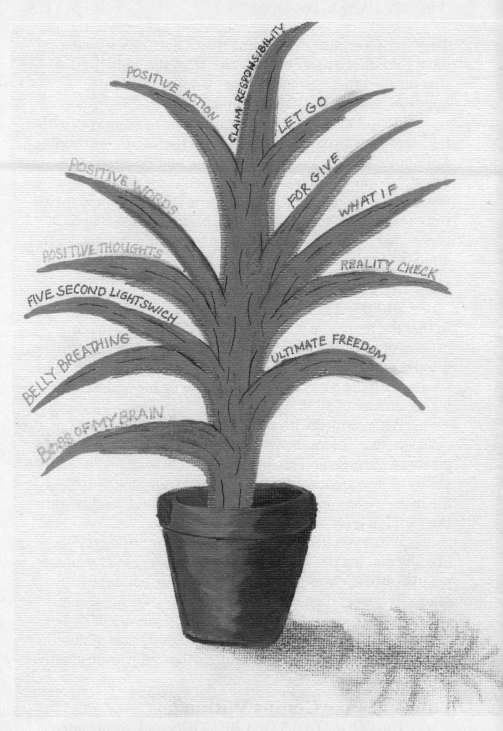

Art is a gift to GOGI from GOGI student Tom Roberson.

we see so much suffering across so many different cultures and peoples? In consideration of this fact, let's take one more look at bravery. Whether the motivation is divine or desperation, the individual may inherit power, often times buried within, to direct and dictate their own life's direction. The TOOLS OF CREATION are powerful, but most effective when combined with the steady practice of all the GOGI Tools.

   In review, the TOOLS OF THE BODY empower you to take control of the physical. TOOLS OF CHOICE permit you to direct your next steps along your journey. TOOLS OF MOVING FORWARD free you from attachments to the past. And, our beloved TOOLS OF CREATION unlock your creative genius to contribute positively to the world in which you live.

   Let's explore each Tool in detail in the following chapters.

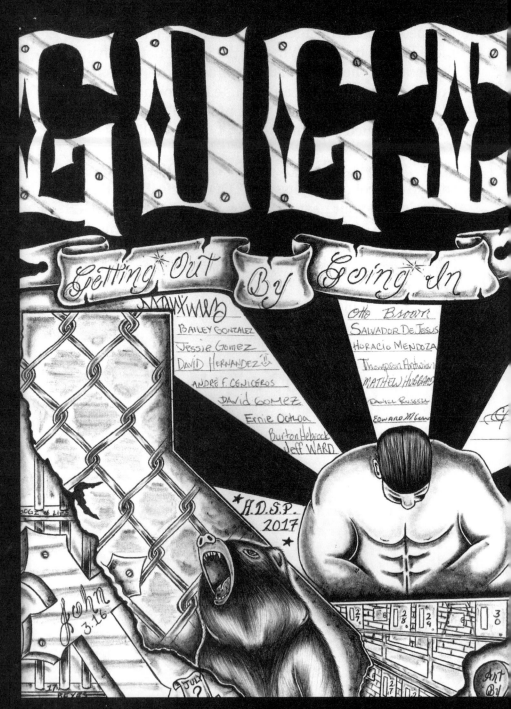

Art is a gift to GOGI from GOGI student Armando Reyes, HDSP.

———————— Chapter 16 ————————

The GOGI Tool
WHAT IF

WHAT IF is part of the set of Tools called TOOLS OF CREATION. This Tool lets you create new outcomes for yourself by taking you out of life's victim seat and putting you in charge of your decisions. You can give everything the WHAT IF all day, every day, so you can see just where your choices are leading you. WHAT IF you signed up for a class? WHAT if you didn't? WHAT IF you made that phone call? WHAT IF you didn't? WHAT IF you reached out to someone in need? WHAT IF you didn't? When you start using WHAT IF for all your choices, you may first notice that most of your choices today are exactly the same as your choices yesterday. How are you expecting a different outcome with the same choices? With this tool, you can give all thoughts, words and actions the WHAT IF and create something different from the past.

There are two ways you can use the Tool WHAT IF. You can use it to play out the likely results of a negative action, or you can use WHAT IF to play out the positive possibilities.

What might be possible if you asked WHAT IF? WHAT IF you went back to school? WHAT IF you created a different affiliation? WHAT IF you joined AA? WHAT IF you attended chapel services? WHAT IF you read positive books? WHAT IF you didn't do the same old things when you got home? WHAT IF you learned to meditate? WHAT IF you began to work out and eat healthy foods each day?

On the other hand, WHAT IF you keep doing what you have always done? WHAT IF you don't do things differently?

Your Future your Way

Many individuals fail to look into the future far enough to get a clear picture of the ripple effect created by each and every decision. As a GOGI Tool, WHAT IF permits you to see into the likely outcome of the future, to get a clear idea about what this one cigarette, this last high, or this next rage episode means.

Each action, as small as it may seem, has a big ripple effect in your future. WHAT IF permits you to slow down your actions long enough to see the future result of your small and seemingly insignificant decisions.

For individuals who struggle with the desire for the pleasure of instant gratification or those who suffer from impulse control challenges, the Tool WHAT IF lifts the fog and lets you instantly see the outcome. You become the master, the controller, the one dictating what is going to happen to you in the future.

This Tool WHAT IF is your peek into the future, and permits you to make your choices accordingly. You get to ask, "WHAT IF I am not my past?"

The cool thing about the Tool WHAT IF is that it permits you to predict the likely future outcome of today's actions. If you witness someone walking into the chapel each day, the eventual outcome will likely be someone with a more religious attitude. If you witness someone pulling out a cigarette each day, the eventual outcome will be someone who hangs out with smokers, thinks about smoking, smells like smoke, and suffers from the inevitable health limitations caused by smoking. If you see someone reading and spending time in the law library, the eventual outcome will be someone who increased their knowledge of law.

WHAT IF is a Tool which gets you out of the immediate desires running rampant in your mind and gets you to play out the scene like a movie script. You can ask yourself, "WHAT IF I do this? Is it negative or positive? WHAT IF I don't do this? What else might I do?".

Taming the Wave

Impulsive, frightened, angry, and depressed people all have a difficult time controlling the immediacy of their feelings. It is often difficult for them to actually see beyond the wave of emotions or opinions far enough to see an outcome.

WHAT IF is a popular Tool for anyone interested in directing their future. By looking into the possible future outcome, by gauging if an action is on the positive or negative path, they are more inclined to overcome the wave of emotions clouding their ability to make positive decisions.

Negative? Positive?

Here is the place where people get tripped up with the Tool WHAT IF. For some reason, they refuse to acknowledge that everything they do (and we mean everything they do) is either negative or positive. One last drink is negative. One last negative statement is negative. One missed AA meeting, one skipped church meeting, one time cheating on an exam, one buying of a counterfeit certificate, one misrepresentation of the truth, is negative.

These small and seemingly insignificant negatives create a hugely negative outcome and they are just like boulders in the way of your success. Boulders, by the way, which are put in place by you.

Here is a question for you to consider. WHAT IF you stop being your only enemy and start using WHAT IF to direct every action of every day? WHAT IF you did not make that poor choice you know only leads downward? WHAT IF enough was truly enough and you got down to the business of making your life a positive creation?

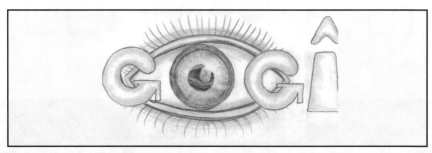

GOGI

INSIGHT

Cameron Mitchell
Cameron Mitchell

WHAT IF

WHAT IF I AM NOT MY PAST?

No to the past = Yes to the future

WHAT IF is a Tool that can be used to predict possible future outcomes. You can predict much of your future with WHAT IF. Here is how:

- POSITIVE OR NEGATIVE? – Is this action positive or negative?

- BEST OR WORST? – What is the possible outcome? What is the worst that can happen? What is the best that can happen?

- POSSIBLE OUTCOME – I clearly see a possible outcome. My choice will lead me in a direction.

- TAKE ACTION– If not a positive direction, I tell myself to pick any other action which is positive.

Your future is predictable. What you do today is creating your future. WHAT IF is a tool you can use to dedicate yourself to a positive outcome. WHAT IF there is a new you emerging, thought by thought, word by word, and action by action?

♥~ Coach Taylor

Art is a gift to GOGI from GOGI student Woody Hartman.

─── Chapter 17 ───

The GOGI Tool
REALITY CHECK

REALITY CHECK is part of the set of Tools called TOOLS OF CREATION. This Tool is your permission to be a flawed human, but does not give you permission to remain in a flawed state. Your TEN STEPS FORWARD and TWO STEPS BACK are still EIGHT STEPS AHEAD. Your two steps back do not mean you are a failure. What it means, when you use REALITY CHECK, is that you acknowledge you really messed up, but you get right back on track by making your very next decision be the most positive decision possible. With REALITY CHECK, you understand that you are not perfect, but you keep moving forward towards perfection with your very next thought, word and action. Your mistakes do not define you, what defines you is how you get back on track once mistakes are made. REALITY CHECK lets you course correct quickly.

The GOGI Tool REALITY CHECK offers you a new way of thinking about change. What often happens is that we make serious promises to stop doing something. We may even do a great job at our new commitment until the bottom falls out of our lives and something terrible happens. Then, somehow, we find ourselves right back into old behavior; or, maybe the bottom doesn't fall out, and somehow we have slipped back into our old habits without even knowing what happened.

Regardless of how we get there, many people throw in the towel and beat themselves up with shame and blame when they relapse into old behavior. Then, having given up, they decide they may as well go on another run and ride this old rodeo all the way out once again.

Stop the Ride

REALITY CHECK permits you to stop the inevitable ride to the bottom by focusing on your successes. Is it terrible that you were backsliding? Yes. But, not as terrible as giving up and letting a mistake or a failure take you all the way down to the bottom once again.

The Tool REALITY CHECK states that ten steps forward and two steps back is still eight steps ahead. Getting back on track as quickly as possible is more important than trying to ignore or just "go with" your failures. You and everyone you know are simply human. Humans are error-prone beings.

Once you accept that learning from errors is an opportunity of the human experience, you can be a little kinder to yourself when you stumble and you can use REALITY CHECK to get back on track quickly. There is no point in trying to be perfect. You will fail at that. There is great accomplishment, however, in not letting your failures or mistakes diminish your commitment to progress.

REALITY CHECK allows you to look at mistakes from the perspective that the mistake does not dictate your future success. With REALITY CHECK, you get right back on track as quickly as possible and keep moving forward.

As with all the GOGI Tools, our interpretation of the actual words are different than the common use of the words. FOR–GIVE, for example, is different than to forgive. As a Tool, CLAIM RESPONSIBILITY is different than to claim responsibility. This is similar to the Tool REALITY CHECK.

Never Perfect always Progress

REALITY CHECK is a Tool for you to use when you backslide, make a mistake, fall off, do something stupid, or are tempted to toss in the towel and live in shame for not being perfect. With the Tool REALITY CHECK, you understand you are not perfect. You will never be perfect.

If perfection is something you attempt to achieve in vain, you may find yourself in a downward spiral of self-hatred sinking lower into bad decisions because you are discouraged with your imperfections.

REALITY CHECK is about not falling victim to the perfection syndrome, but, rather, being focused on getting back on the right path as quickly as possible so the damage of weak actions are as minimal as possible.

Your Life Raft

As a Tool, REALITY CHECK is to be used as a life raft in the sea of bad decisions. It is your escape route from needing one more rodeo ride. It is your ticket back on the right track, back to the positive. REALITY CHECK does not focus on your mistakes, but focuses on how much good you have done up to the time of your mistake. Then, setting aside the mistakes, REALITY CHECK has you focus on getting right back on track with the use of your GOGI Tools.

Remember, if you take ten steps forward and then fall back a couple steps, you are still eight steps ahead. And, if you take ten steps forward and eleven steps back, at least you know how to step forward. There is no room for self victimization with REALITY CHECK because you are not going to sit around and beat yourself up with negative self talk. With this Tool, you are able to pick yourself up and take that next right action.

Delicate Dance of Change

REALITY CHECK is the most awesome Tool because change is rarely linear. It is almost always a delicate dance of backwards and forwards, inching your way into a new reality. Of course, it is easier if we just walk the path forward, but, alas, humans are humans and it appears as if we prefer to learn things the hard way until we decide the easy way is... easier. REALITY CHECK permits us to create the easier route to change in the dance of creating a positive life.

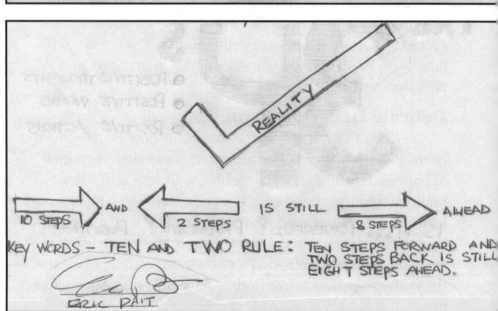

REALITY CHECK

TEN AND TWO RULE

Ten steps forward and two steps back is still eight steps ahead.

REALITY CHECK is your Tool for when you mess up, make a mistake, or fall victim to temptation. The GOGI Tool REALITY CHECK also helps you have compassion for weaknesses in others. It works like this:

- FACT – I messed up.

- PROGRESS – There are many times I don't mess up. I have made progress. I have done really well, better than I have in the past. One mistake does not erase all the good. I understand my good is still my good.

- BACK ON TRACK– Right now, this moment, I can choose more good, adding to my list of good things I have done. I commit to POSITIVE ACTIONS right now. I am back on track.

REALITY CHECK is the perfect Tool if shame, self-loathing, embarrassment, and discouragement have been your pattern. You are not and will never be perfect, so get over it and just commit to being better today than yesterday, and better tomorrow than today. ♥~ *Coach Taylor*

Art is a gift to GOGI from GOGI student Erickson.

—————————— Chapter 18 ——————————
The GOGI Tool
ULTIMATE FREEDOM

ULTIMATE FREEDOM is part of the set of Tools called TOOLS OF CREATION. This Tool is least obvious of Tools because it is used to create a way of moving through your day and not necessarily a Tool you pull out when something breaks down. When you use your Tool ULTIMATE FREEDOM, you are deciding that your decisions are helping you be of service. You do this by being positive; that is a service to others. You do this by being helpful; that is a service to others. You do this by being a safe distance from harm; that is a service to others. When you use ULTIMATE FREEDOM, you realize that you are important as a walking, talking potential solution to any and every problem. As a walking and talking solution, you are living a life of service. THAT is the ultimate use of the tool ULTIMATE FREEDOM

ULTIMATE FREEDOM as a GOGI Tool is pretty simple. Until you are living each and every day of your life in service of making the world a better place, you are not truly free. If you are living for your own gratification, you will eventually be unhappy.

If you are living your life to "get more" and "have more," then you will eventually experience disappointment and dissatisfaction. ULTIMATE FREEDOM as a GOGI Tool, helps us realize our freedom is not determined by physical freedom.

ULTIMATE FREEDOM is what can be experienced when you focus your life's actions toward helping others and living humbly in service of those who struggle and those who are blinded by the need for "things" or maintaining a certain image.

Live with no Regrets

When, at the end of the day, you can review your activities and decisions and count numerous times that you brought a smile or hope to another individual, that is when you can be certain that your use of this Tool of ULTIMATE FREEDOM is part of every day life.

Living your life in the humble service of making your corner of the world a nicer, cleaner, and kinder place, permits your life to be filled with learning, sharing, and loving.

When we get close to the time we leave this earth, we will naturally reflect on important things that define our life. In speaking with thousands of individuals who suffer from illnesses that take their lives, each individual speaks about relationships, learning, sharing, and communication as being most important.

A dying individual simply does not talk about big houses, new cars and all the distractions which are promoted in our culture as the route to happiness. A dying individual will tell you about love, regrets in love, the importance of the small things in life, the small acts of kindness. They often speak of regrets.

So, while we have thousands upon thousands of individuals who, on their death beds, have told us what is truly important, why is it that we focus on the superficial collection of things we cannot take with us when we leave this earth?

Your Freedom

Knowing this, if you live each day as if it were to be your last day, your focus would likely be more on positive connections with those nearby.

Using the ULTIMATE FREEDOM Tool gets us back on track. Using ULTIMATE FREEDOM, permits us to focus on being someone who is respected and loved, an individual who will be missed when we leave this earth.

The Tool ULTIMATE FREEDOM makes internal freedom possible for each one of us. The other GOGI Tools are simply Tools to get us in a position to live a life of daily use of the tool ULTIMATE FREEDOM. By using your Tools and being of service at least one time each day, you are inching your way to toward truly living.

Service as a Key

There is likely no greater internal joy than living your life in the service of those in need. But (and there is always a but), this cannot be done until you are in the mental space and emotional space to actually be of service. If you are not prepared to be of service, then the service you provide may actually be measured and counted by you, and debts are accumulated in your mind. You are still in a form of a prison.

The Tool ULTIMATE FREEDOM is certainly not for the faint of heart or those clouded with emotional requirements to be acknowledged or rewarded. The Tool ULTIMATE FREEDOM is about doing something for others which probably will never be noticed. Or, even better yet, doing something positive for others who have harmed, hurt or caused you great pain. Be of service to anyone, regardless of their actions towards you. That will give you a freedom few others experience.

Simple Freedom

This may be quite a heavy concept to grasp so let's keep it simple. Let's keep it to the daily actions you choose in your life. By committing to doing one act of kindness for another human being which is not seen nor heard by others, you are laying the foundation for a life filled with the freedom for which we all secretly strive.

We all want to be internally free of sadness, anger, codependency, dependence, depression, addiction, rage, despair, hopelessness, illness, etc. A single true balm for these feelings, a lasting healing, comes from the daily practice of the Tool ULTIMATE FREEDOM.

Try to picture yourself being of service by roaming the country in long robes and picking up trash along the freeways for the rest of your life. Begin to think about how you can use ULTIMATE FREEDOM today.

Pick out one little, seemingly insignificant thing you can do to make the life of someone else just a little bit better. Do that thing without any expectation of acknowledgment, no reward, no accolades. Do it unnoticed. Do it, just to do it. If someone says thank you or notices you, pick out something else you can do where there is no reward, no "thank you" attached.

Maybe it is as simple as picking up a piece of trash, or making the row of books a little more organized. Maybe it is keeping your bedding tidy and nice to look at, or teaching someone to read. Maybe it is writing a letter to an English teacher of your high school, sharing inspiring words with the students of that school.

Whatever it is, pick one way in which you can be of service. Fill your life with these acts and freedom will be your lasting life experience, regardless of the inevitable challenges you will face.

Art is a gift to GOGI from GOGI student Fernando Moreno.

ULTIMATE FREEDOM

BEING FREE IS UP TO ME

Living a life of service gives me ULTIMATE FREEDOM.

ULTIMATE FREEDOM is a "state of being" just as much as it is a Tool. Here is how to practice the Tool ULTIMATE FREEDOM each and every day:

① FREE DAY – I begin my day in freedom from anything which might hold me back. Today, I am of positive service to my world.

② SERVICE – I will do one thing for which I accept no money and will accumulate no favors. If possible, I will do this act of service without anyone knowing.

③ JOY – I will slow my thoughts enough to feel the joy in my heart that only comes from doing good deeds today.

④ SMILE – Even if things are terrible in my life right now, I will smile each and every time I think about ULTIMATE FREEDOM and my service to my world.

⑤ END EACH DAY – I end my day by reviewing times I used ULTIMATE FREEDOM, when I was in service. Being of service sets me internally free!

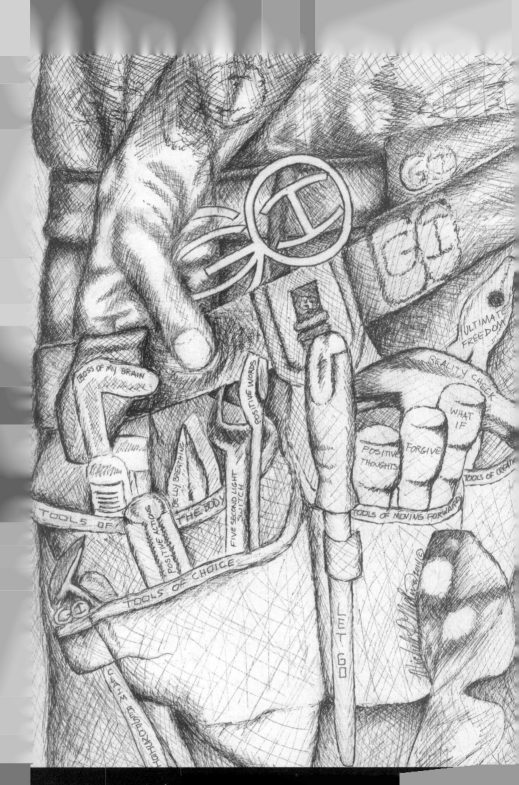

Art is a

Section Two
The **GOGI Way**

GOGI TO ME IS LIKE ROSES THAT GREW FROM CONCRETE

My signature _Ricardo Veyna_
Print your name _Ricardo Veyna_

──────── Chapter 19 ────────
The Promise of a Positive Culture

Some individuals enjoy understanding the pieces and parts of things, the workings and makings of whatever it is that draws their interest. Others don't care about the details and simply know what they like based on other factors. And, some base their interest on scientifically proven results or other documents.

For many years, GOGI sent to GOGI Students a form called "Your Opinion Matters." In this one-page document, we asked several thousands of students over a period of ten years to share their opinions and experiences of their own GOGI Journey. This helped us remain on track with voices we were striving to hear and the Culture we were in the process of creating.

The Origin of GOGI

One question on this form was related to the origins of GOGI. It asked if it mattered to them that the GOGI Tools were created by prisoners and for prisoners. Most individuals felt the origins of the GOGI Tools to be important, that it was the foundation for the future of GOGI. For others, they did not care either way. Others stated that they liked the GOGI Tools, but did not feel particularly warm and fuzzy knowing prisoners came up with them. For these individuals, they preferred to believe that their beloved "Coach Taylor" was behind it all and they were not a set of Tools created by society's "undesirables" or whatever label they might have used.

The point is each of us develops our own unique way of coming to understand our world. For me, at this time in my life, my motivating factor was self-preservation. Way back in 2002, I was of the mind-set that if I didn't figure out this thing called "life" pretty quickly, then I did not want it. When sitting with the prisoners during the early years of GOGI, I was more so coming from a place of desperation than a selfless act of philanthropy.

GOGI Sounded Funny

Sitting with the men in prison, I did not care that the word "GOGI" sounded funny. Nor did I care that men in prison uniforms were giving me better information and better Tools than those I learned in the school classroom or from well-meaning parents. I did not care that I was putting one hand on my belly and one hand on my chest and hoping that I could learn the Tool BELLY BREATHING. I did not care about anything more than there was a small part of me that wanted to live, but a bigger part of me that knew that if I did not find some answers soon, I would not.

I am sharing this with you because this section of the book contains details for the curious at heart. It is not information for the desperate or distraught, as I was. There would have been no way I would have read even one page of this section until I believed I was swimming and not drowning in a relentless sea of despair. This section of the book is for those who are not sinking, not thinking about an Earth-exit-plan, and those who are no longer stuck in a loop of self harm from which they cannot escape.

The Basics

This section of this book contains a bit of GOGI's history, our origins as a Community of like minded individuals, and basic things like how you say G.O.G.I. as a word. (Hint: most new GOGI students say it Go-gee, like "G-wiz." But, to say it correctly it sounds like Go-Ghee, not Go-G.)

If all the information in this section seems to be boring, redundant, and unnecessary to your own quest for internal freedom, feel free to skip ahead to a section that may serve you better. There is no harm in passing up the next several chapters and possibly glancing through them later. When you are able to live your life with access to the GOGI Tools, you will discover that all of life is a buffet and you can pick and choose those aspects that nourish and feed you. You do not need to eat everything on your plate. It is more important to enjoy and feel the benefits of what you eat and not quite as important for you to stuff yourself with the unnecessary.

Turn a Few Pages

If a particular page does not have a mini-header that appeals to you (those little titles we have added to make it easier to skim through), please turn a few more pages. My apologies for not doing a better job of organizing the information into a format or style that is a bit more readable. "Real" books have "real" publishers and real teams of editors who sift through an author's materials until the final copy is unrecognizable to the first submitted draft.

At GOGI, we have none of that support, which also means you are getting the raw materials, the real thing, the unfiltered version and probably a lot of typos and grammatical errors. For some, this might be terribly irritating, for which I have regrets. But, there is one solid reason for our autonomy during the formative years of developing what I believe is the "Culture" of GOGI. At GOGI, you are getting a chunk of sugar cane instead of the white refined granules you may put into your morning coffee. You can process the sugar cane chunk exactly as you wish; we will not serve you the granules.

Raw and Unfiltered

Raw and unfiltered is how all things GOGI have evolved. This is the promise of its sustainability; deep roots embedded in GOGI will survive a drought, should there be one in the future.

As I write these words, I am sitting at an old sewing

machine stand from the 1800's that now serves as a desk that is the perfect height for my needs. When the desk was created, there was no vision for its use more than 100 years down the road, but, alas, the desk has a new and important function. So, too, will GOGI, the GOGI Tools, the GOGI Journey, and living "The GOGI Way" evolve into something unplanned but beautiful and practical.

While the simplified GOGI Tools were created to serve those individuals with the greatest investment in finding freedom, my sense is that long after I exit this earthly plain, the GOGI Culture that emerged through this organic creation will remain available to bless the lives of others for generations to come.

It is my Hope

Enjoy this section if you will, pass it by if it does not serve you. However you manage any part of this book is yours to decide. Simply know, it is my hope that you embrace and understand one thing. Every word written is being offered from the most sincere part of me and the most sincere part of those tens of thousands of prisoners who have found some form of freedom as a result of the details you may find herein.

A Promise from my Heart

There are times I wish every living being could experience the joy I have felt since the moment I learned how to apply the GOGI Tools into my life. I sincerely hope you feel a glimmer of this joy as you apply the Tools to decisions you make, and goals you set for yourself.

Then, that little glimmer of joy will have room within your heart and soul to expand. This expansion will fuel even more positive decisions, and you may find yourself smiling, even when it seems there is not much to smile about.

Each and every human wants to contribute positively to the world around them, even if they deny this with great fervor. Every human wants to have a positive impact. Every human seeks the freedom to create a sense of internal freedom. Imagine a Culture where individuals obtaining this internal freedom is the norm. That is the GOGI Culture.

With your GOGI Tools, you will have more of a chance to fulfill your life's dream than ever before. Having simple Tools you can use in every aspect of your life, puts you in control of your future. You are only limited by the choices you make, not by the circumstances in which you find yourself.

what do you do when you are standing on a prison yard with over a thousand other men and you make a phone call and you hear your fathers voice for the first time in months and you find out he is homeless and drunk.
You belly breathe.

What do you do when you find out that he is choosing alcohol over his own family
You remind yourself that you are the boss of your brain.

What do you do when he tells you that he doesn't have long to live and he isn't going to stop drinking even if it means spending less time with his family.
You use the What if tool.

what do you do when he says he hasn't been there for you your whole life, and he most likely won't be because he would rather drink.
You forgive.

What do you do when you start blaming yourself for your father being an alcoholic?
You Let Go!

What do you do when your eyes fill up with tears and you want to make someone else hurt as much as you are hurting that very moment?
You use the 5 second Light Switch

What do you do when people can see your pain and how hurt you are and ask you what is going on.
You use positive thoughts, words, and actions.

Besides thanking God for Coach Taylor and the 12 tools of GOGI I now have to make better decisions, claim responsibility

BOMB

Boss of My brain

Art is a gift to GOGI from the art collection of Coach Baca.

——————— Chapter 20 ———————
GOGI and You

A Simple Way of Looking at Life

This idea of "The GOGI Way" often has people confused. They question if GOGI is a "program," a "religion," a 12-step program, or a club of some sort. GOGI is none of those things. It doesn't matter what program or religion you might follow when you study The GOGI Tools. It does not matter your race, age, size, sex, culture, or intellect. The fact is, living your life "The GOGI Way" can help you make more positive decisions.

Everything gets Better with GOGI

The GOGI philosophy is more than a set of simple Tools. GOGI is, also, a way of looking at your life that helps you become better at anything you choose to do. The GOGI philosophy is similar to, and is consistent with, core human values, which are at the foundation of most religions and efforts aiding in the improvement of the human condition.

Is NOW your Time?

What might your life be like if you truly had the power to make lasting changes? Who are you without the drama, chaos and desperation of poor decisions?

WHAT IF you are not your past? Rather, WHAT IF you can learn to, slowly, but surely, learn a new way of living? WHAT IF now is YOUR time for change? Next time you are doubting yourself, try this: close your eyes and just imagine the possibility of lasting change.

You may come to realize change IS possible, as soon as you realize the possibility. Ask yourself, "WHAT IF I used my GOGI Tools and became part of the solution?"

Genuinely Happy

It is said that people who live "The GOGI Way" by making more positive decisions seem to look happier, seem to have a glow about them, and display a happiness which comes from within. This is true. Happiness on the inside will eventually find a way into your daily life experience.

The GOGI philosophy helps you be a better person, creating internal happiness that is obvious to others. The GOGI philosophy is not about polishing the outside, but rather empowering you to do a reconstruction project from the inside out. This internal happiness is true and right for all humans and is not limited to a select group of people.

You, too, can incorporate GOGI Tools into your daily life and you, too, can begin to reap the benefits of living your life The GOGI Way. Simply choose to use GOGI Tools any time you need a nudge in the right direction.

The GOGI Vision

As the first volunteer for GOGI, I began to envision the future of the organization even before it was anything more than a weekly class held for few prisoners. In one of my first interviews I remember saying,

"Early on, I would have dreams during my sleep about GOGI. I began to see men and women, not with tattoos of gang affiliations, wearing GOGI leadership shirts and carrying GOGI books on their way to lead meetings in other housing units. I saw these leaders claiming their position as productive members of society dedicated to being of service to others.

I saw the antithesis of a gang violence culture; I saw an emerging service-oriented culture, a GOGI gang-for-good, where millions of GOGI-affiliated individuals could live their lives in humble service to others, helping others make positive choices with their lives.

In my dream, I saw millions of people united, not by their gender, their color or religion, but by the core values that link us all together. That was my dream, and in my waking moments, GOGI consumed my every thought.

It seemed so simple, the solution to the problem of generational incarceration and recidivism; GOGI was the easiest way to deliver core human values and simple decision making tools that united all individuals for good works in our communities.

By empowering individuals to set good examples for others, we create a sustainable system which requires nothing more than the willingness of the individual to self-correct."

True to the original vision, the GOGI Culture has, and will, continue to expand. The simplicity of the Tools, which emerged from the most complex forms of imprisonment, is a testament to the power of the individual when they become focused on being of service.

Art is a gift to GOGI from GOGI student Uriel Magana Contreras.

Art is a gift to GOGI from GOGI student Justin Allee.

How does GOGI Support Sobriety?

Our volunteers state that in volunteering to share their GOGI Tools, their sobriety is more secure. They state that in being of service through volunteering to share their GOGI Tools, they are reminded of the fragility of their own freedom.

What Changes First, the System or the Person?

Most individuals believe the problem is in the system; that the system needs to change before they can find freedom. It may feel that way; as if change is impossible when you are trapped in an environment that is hostile or demeaning.

It may feel as if nothing can be done until there is enough space for change to occur or until someone acknowledges your positive efforts. This is a common trap, waiting for permission, approval, or acknowledgement, or a revamp of the system before you can change.

When you believe the system is the only problem, you render yourself paralyzed, you are unable to think outside the box, and you most certainly are not practicing the GOGI Tool BOSS OF MY BRAIN. The truth is that no one can limit what goes on in your head. You can change before the system, any system, does.

Changing the System from the Inside Out

During one discussion about change in a GOGI group, one man boldly stated, "Who are we kidding? We aren't going to change the system. Not from in here. We have no credibility. First, we need to change what's in here," he said, pointing to his heart.

This man understood the power of the GOGI philosophy. The goal of GOGI is to provide powerful and success-guaranteed Tools for positive decision making in order to change the system from the inside out. As the discussion continued among this group of men, they clearly agreed that if one man could change internally and get out of the system, then others could do it as well. The GOGI student believes in and supports the internal change of the individual as being the prerequisite to a systemic change.

A Key to Lasting Change

The key to lasting change is for you to use your GOGI Tools while keeping focused on the kind of life you are creating for yourself. When you can keep your eyes focused on the kind of life you want, you overcome the daily obstacles far more easily.

Living your life "The GOGI Way" is possible, no matter how entrenched into another lifestyle or affiliation you might be. Having a family that for generations could not avoid jail cells, drugs and harming others, does not mean you are limited in your choices for your own life.

Change Is Inevitable

Remember, change is inevitable, and your survival in life and your success in love and learning are dependent upon your ability to grow and change.

GOGI students understand that even GOGI, as an emerging culture or way of living, will wither and die if it does not remain responsive to the need for flexibility, change, and growth.

Change will happen and it is our response to this inevitable change which determines our destiny.

Comfort Zone

The truth is, change is often uncomfortable, and at times we give up before we have made that change a part of our daily life. It's like going to Disneyland, getting inside, and then turning around and walking out because we don't recognize anyone there. We give up before the fun starts.

GOGI permits you to use your Tools to get inside the amusement park of life long enough to start having fun in your new self-created lifestyle. That is why GOGI suggests you focus on the life you want to create, you pick your Tool or Tools, and you begin to live "The GOGI Way," by making positive decisions each and every day.

It will take a huge, unwavering commitment to muscle your way through the natural discomfort which comes with change, but it can be done. And, knowing that there are more and more people learning, loving and living "The GOGI Way", this journey should seem less solo.

Heaven or Hell?

There is an old saying that goes something like this: "I would rather be in hell with my friends than in heaven with a bunch of strangers." That holds a lot of truth for nearly everyone. Who wants to go to an amusement park alone? We want to have fun with our friends, our familiar relationships, and those who have been through a lot of struggle with us. We don't want to change alone.

What part of that way of being may be holding you back? Many individuals are fearful of change, they don't trust something new, different, or out of reach. WHAT IF you realized that every person you now know was, at one time, a stranger?

During your life you have met and associated with toddlers, kindergartners, elementary kids, high school age kids, young adults, and adults. You have met thousands of humans of different ages and experiences. In every case, at some point they were unknown.

You are the Solution

When you understand and apply the GOGI Tools to your decision process in life, you will find that YOU are the solution. It may be impossible to believe you are the solution at this moment, but believe it or not, you hold a potential solution for your situation. You even hold within you the solution for your community.

When you use the GOGI Tools, and when you "Live The GOGI Way", you will find that everyone and everything is better because of all the positivity you have to offer. You ARE the solution, you just might not know it yet.

Mi Escudo

GOT

Por Vida

Art is a gift to GOGI from GOGI student Armondo Sandoval.

————— Chapter 21 —————
Your **GOGI** Practice

What Does Getting Out by Going In Mean?

Getting Out by Going In (GOGI) is a non-profit organization and volunteer-driven group of citizens who believe that humans can, and do make positive decisions when their desire for change is combined with positive decision making tools. Getting Out by Going In is way more than just an organization.

Getting Out by Going In is also something you can do, turning inward for answers to get out of old self-created prisons. GOGI means getting out of your mental prison by going inside yourself for the answers.

When someone is "Getting Out by Going In," they are choosing to utilize their unlimited potential for positive decision making by using the GOGI Tools to help them change, grow, and create opportunities. GOGI, as an organization, is dedicated and committed to teaching simple Tools that help a majority of people make better decisions.

The GOGI Way is one which empowers you to Get Out of old behavior by Going Into yourself for the solutions. The GOGI philosophy believes that if you take your focus off the problems around you and focus your efforts on fixing the problems within you, you will soon realize that there are fewer problems.

By turning your focus inward, you will also identify simple solutions to those seemingly out-of-control problems which once kept you up at night or caused worry during the day.

Art is a gift to GOGI from GOGI student Charles Hennecke.

How Do I Say GOGI?

GOGI is pronounced Go-Ghee, with two hard "G" sounds. It is not pronounced Go-"G". To say it correctly, GOGI rhymes with Yogi, like Yogi Bear, or a hoagie sandwich.

What Does Getting Out by Going In Do?

The non-profit organization, Getting Out by Going In (GOGI), provides simple Tools to anyone interested in positive decision making. This book and other GOGI materials encourage everyone to learn the GOGI Tools and apply these Tools in their lives in as many ways as possible.

How Do I Use the Tools?

One single Tool can make all the difference in your life. You don't need to master all of the GOGI Tools. We have learned from many prisoners that simply using one Tool in every stressful situation is enough to change your life for the better. You have a full toolkit, but might only use a handful of Tools.

Here's an easy way to use the Tools: pick a favorite tool and practice it constantly throughout the day, under every circumstance, establishing that Tool in your mind and body as the routine way you handle things.

This will enable you to pull this Tool out of your Toolbox when it is most needed, without having to think about it. When you practice just one Tool often enough, it becomes automatic as a reaction or response, resulting in a more positive outcome.

Which Tool is Best for Me?

Some individuals get overwhelmed with having multiple Tools to help them change. All of the Tools may seem like too many. Trying to pick just the right Tool for each situation can get confusing.

Here is a thought for you. Almost everyone who uses the GOGI Tools say they really only use one Tool. They will say they know all the Tools, but they have their favorite Tool

Just One Tool

The fact is, all you need is one Tool. If you did nothing more than go through this book only reading the information about one Tool, and became skilled at that Tool only, you will have all the power you need to change every part of yourself that no longer benefits you. One Tool is all it takes to make significant changes.

So, if you feel overwhelmed, or if you are unsure of your ability to remain on track, just hold tightly to that one Tool that you pick to be your favorite.

Write it down and put it in your sock. Keep it posted near your bed. Keep a copy in your pocket. Create as many visible reminders of your favorite Tool and your Tool will not let you down. Call on it regularly and it will work for you.

If you get bored with that favorite Tool, pick another. You can switch it up any time you like.

What is the Best Way to Learn GOGI?

The best way to learn The GOGI Philosophy is any way you are able to learn GOGI. If there is a PowerUp! Community Meeting, join the group. If there are no groups, you can start one with a peer who may welcome a positive support system. If you do not feel comfortable in a group setting, study on your own according to the GOGI Calendar of Study and you will never be alone.

You can share what you learn in letters and conversations with others. Discuss what you read with others. The more ways you get GOGI in your life, the easier your changes will be. The best way to learn GOGI is whichever way is right for you, just make your learning happen. Do what works for you.

For some individuals, learning is easiest in a structured course method. GOGI offers many of those options and we ask donors to help us keep the cost of published soft bound courses as low as possible.

I Don't Understand!!!!

There are many people who may get frustrated with many things that are taught in this book. They say it is too much or too confusing. You may be one of those people. You may find that a lot of words are confusing, or there may be things you wish could be told to you in person so you could understand better. You are not alone.

Before you walk away thinking this book is not for you, please do this one thing. Please pick out ANYTHING in the book that you DO understand. Pick out a picture, a poem, or a quote. Pick out ANYTHING and just focus on that.

Just understand every bit of that one thing. Study it. Really look at it. Share it with someone else.

Hang On

If you understand one thing in this book, that is powerful. Hang on to that one thing. Then, once you feel you really understand that one thing really well, pick out one more thing—one more picture, one more poem, one more page that catches your interest.

You can have this GOGI book for many years and still not understand everything. That is good because you can always grow with GOGI. Just come to understand one thing at a time and you will be doing a great job in your GOGI studies.

WHAT IF

This is where the Tool WHAT IF comes into play. WHAT IF you are not your past? WHAT IF what you are right now is not all you are meant to be? WHAT IF your low self esteem, disastrous track record or one big time mistake was not the only road map to your future? WHAT IF there really are other options?

When you consider another possibility, you are opening the door for a new reality. If you never consider something different, you will never be able to walk through that door.

What do you Really Want?

In your mind, you must create a clear idea of the kind of life you might want if you were able to make changes. This is very easy when you have examples, when you meet or read about those who have made changes, or when you surround yourself with others who are making changes.

Start Small - Get Big Results

There are varying levels of success when applying the GOGI Tools to life's inevitable challenges. You may never be perfect at everything, but students of "The GOGI Way" find that they are better at most things when they consider their GOGI Toolbox as a resource for their efforts.

Start small when learning your Tools. Think big picture, but start with the small actions. Monitor your use of just one Tool over time, as this awareness will encourage you to continue, even when facing insurmountable challenges. Focus on your future, being mindful that each thought, word, and action today is what will get you to your goal.

Stay Involved

Remember, your GOGI Tools are in addition to, not a replacement for, your other efforts. Continue to involve yourself in any and every activity where positive people gather. If there is a group of individuals wanting to be of service to their community, you can bet they are using their GOGI Tools, even if they have a different name for them. A Culture is created when it becomes second nature, or a norm. Use of the GOGI Tools can become your new norm, a new Culture you can share with the world around you.

Where Do I Study GOGI?

Reading, writing and discussing are all part of learning GOGI Tools, so dedicate time to integrating GOGI into these activities. You can run the track with GOGI on your mind, you can walk the yard with GOGI in your thoughts. You can climb the stairs, mop the floor, or even count the bricks on the wall while learning and practicing your GOGI Tools.

Most of all, practicing GOGI Tools will permit the tools to become automatic in helping you make positive decisions. Don't stop learning how to live "The GOGI Way" once you finish reading this book. Reading a book is not living The GOGI Way. Even if you are doing your GOGI study in a course or workshop format, that is just a first step. Living The GOGI Way is a lifelong learning opportunity.

You Don't Understand

Many individuals like the sound of changing their lives, but when it comes down to it, they will say, "You don't understand. It is not that easy."

That is correct. It is not THAT easy, but it is easier than you might perceive, especially when you have real Tools to help you make positive decisions.

I Can't Look Weak

Most people remain stuck in a situation because they don't want to fail if they try something new. And, worse yet, if they do try something new, they won't risk looking weak or soft with their new change. This way of thinking will keep you stuck. Even if you are tired, you chose not to risk change because the unknown is often more difficult to accept than the misery to which you are accustomed.

If this describes you, there is a simple solution. Start small. Start your change on the inside, where no one will see. Work on POSITIVE THOUGHTS and swapping out the old thoughts for new ones. No one can call you "weak" because no one can read your mind. Work on BELLY BREATHING. No one can call you "weak" just because your belly moves up and down instead of your chest. Study BOSS OF MY BRAIN. No one can call you "weak" if you ask yourself what part of your brain is in charge. Only you will know you are strong in your internal change.

There are millions of ways you can begin the process of long-term change and not risk your "reputation", friendships, affiliations, family, or safety. If you don't have the ability or the environment to make big changes, that is fine. Start with the small ones, the ones that only you will know. There is plenty of room in your life to be a better version of yourself and not upset anyone else.

One small change at a time may not seem like much. It may not seem to be important, or enough. The funny thing is, over time you may realize, it was the small changes which mattered most.

Follow the Rules

Regardless of how you study your GOGI, make sure you follow the rules. Following the rules of the community or facility as well as, those set forth by GOGI is of utmost importance in your GOGI work. A person who studies GOGI takes a positive approach and is always striving for the "big win" for everyone. The goal in every situation is for all individuals to become more positive. GOGI students call it "Living The GOGI Way," which is a way of living that respects the rules and obeys all laws and sees all people as valuable and important.

GOGI is not a Program

Know this, GOGI, itself, is not a program, although people have studied GOGI in a program format. GOGI is studied by individuals in drug treatment programs and by those who are active in Twelve Step studies. People have included GOGI to enhance their religious studies, meditation, or yoga studies. The GOGI Tools are studied by educators and mediators as a communication tool.

The GOGI Tools are often referred to in other programs and groups. The GOGI Tools can be studied by the individual in their own way, at their own pace. However, GOGI has courses and curricula to support a formal program format and provides certificates when formal course materials are used.

While GOGI Tools are universal, the study of the GOGI Tools is not intended to be a replacement for programs or groups to which you may already belong. GOGI is an additional positive reinforcement, not a substitution. The GOGI Tools as a study is not a replacement for anything... except poor decision making.

Keep up with your programs, continue your spiritual and religious journey, continue your studies, follow through with your commitments, and steadily work toward your goals. Just know that in each of these areas, you can take your GOGI Tools along with you and you will find increased levels of success in all of your endeavors.

Why the Fuss about GOGI?

So, you might be wondering, "What is all the fuss about the GOGI Tools and what makes them so special?" The Tools are so simple that when tested among kindergarten children in Compton, California, each child in an overcrowded classroom could actually perform the instructions of the tools and they smiled when they realized how simple they were to learn. Why the fuss? The fuss is about finally learning simple Tools which can help ANYONE make better decisions.

But...

No buts about it. Unless you are content with your life as it is, enough already. Enough disappointment. Enough lies. Enough empty promises. Enough tears. Enough misery. Enough hurting others. Enough manipulation. Enough of being ashamed of your decisions and the outcomes and posturing as if you have it all going on. You don't have it going on. If you have a slew of excuses, then it is likely you have nothing going on but the same old worn road of misery that costs all of us too much money, too much pain, and too much suffering. As a student of GOGI, you become part of the solution.

It's the System's Fault

The number one lie that might keep you stuck and in the position of a victim is that it's the system's fault. If you are in prison, you are where you are because someone was able to state that you did something which the majority of citizens have decided is "against the law." Enough of letting the government spend way too much money on keeping you locked up simply because you didn't play by the rules or you had friends who chose not to play by the game of life rules defined by those who have the power to make those decisions. Get over it. Stop letting them win by default. Help change the rules if you don't like them. Be the solution.

Wow, that's Heavy!

Realizing you are the solution may feel like a heavy burden. It's not the systems fault? Wow, that's heavy, but so is the burden of building more prisons to lock people away. Do you realize that at the time this book was printed, the United States had a bigger budget for prisons than for schools? Until more people make better decisions, those in power have all the excuses in the world to build more ways to try and stop them.

The Value in Repetition

To be good at anything, you must do it over and over again. Now that you have made it through the book, you are encouraged to turn right back to the cover and start again, knowing that each time you read this book you will gain new and more powerful insights into your own positive decision making skills.

Study with Heightened Interest

Really look at each page. Read every word written with great interest. The second reading will prove to be much more powerful than the first. And then, when you get to the end of the book again, you can read it yet another time. Being persistent and consistent with your GOGI studies will help you build skills to live "The GOGI Way."

Why Do GOGI Students Succeed?

At GOGI, we believe that each individual has the answers inside their heart, mind, and soul, and we believe that daily use of the GOGI Tools will help you find those answers. We believe most people want to be good, they just may not have learned early on how to make positive decisions. At GOGI, we have discovered the key to lasting change is to unlock the prison within to give freedom and power to answers buried deep within the heart and soul of the individual. We empower the individual to find the answers we believe you are capable of discovering within yourself. GOGI teaches that each individual can be their own expert. This concept is easier to learn with Tools discovered by individuals who, personally, know this to be true.

Too Much Information

Repetition of the GOGI Tools is found throughout the pages of this book. You might begin to think you are drowning in an ocean of GOGI information.

Whenever you feel like it is too much information, just turn to one page, just one page which has meaning for you, and focus on that page.

Read it again and again

We each have different ways of learning. You will instinctively know how to learn in your own unique way. This may mean you draw GOGI Tools, sing GOGI Tools songs, dance GOGI moves, yoga GOGI Tools, read GOGI, dream GOGI, talk or teach GOGI Tools. You do what you need to get the Tools into your daily operating system. You do GOGI your way.

What are the Obstacles?

In addition to the temptation to resort to old behavior and old choices, there may be inherent solitude in the process of change. The pattern of failure to change goes like this:

1) You decide you want to change;
2) You start to use your Tools;
3) Your friends wonder what is wrong with you;
4) They wonder why you think you are better than them.

If that is not exactly your particular cycle, take a moment to write down the pattern which has unfolded in your life.

How do I become GOGI?

Anyone, anywhere, who practices the GOGI Tools is considered part of the growing GOGI Community and a student of GOGI. Some people are born knowing how to use the GOGI Tools, because they have an environment that supports the natural use of these Tools. Some people are taught these Tools by family or friends, or through self-help study. Others must learn the GOGI Tools much later in life. The point is, you can always "be" GOGI; all you need to do is put the Tools of GOGI into practice in your daily life.

If I am GOGI, What do I do?

As a member of the GOGI Community, you seek to strengthen the positive qualities in every individual with whom you come into contact, by your example of using the GOGI Tools.

As a GOGI student, you do not need to fix anyone. Rather than focus on what is wrong on the outside of you, you live your life as an example of how to incorporate the GOGI Tools into your daily living. In being an example, others feel inspired to change on their own and at their own pace. You use your Tool LET GO to keep from needing them to understand and change at your pace. You simply live a GOGI life and let others take care of themselves while you provide an example of how it is done.

As a member of the growing GOGI Community, you do not use your position as a GOGI member to manipulate or control; instead, you are a shining example of generosity and you encourage diversity in your groups and study. You give of your knowledge freely because you understand the Tool ULTIMATE FREEDOM and you experience the joy that comes from living a life of service.

Remarkable GOGI

It's remarkable that something as simple as a set of positive decision making tools can make such a profound difference in the lives of millions of individuals. The GOGI Way of making decisions adds value to your life. It is a way of seeing and being in the world which lets you create your life experience from within.

Through your use of the GOGI Tools, you may find the ability to change your world from the inside out. The best part of all is that The GOGI Way can be a way of making decisions just the way you need them to fortify your positive life.

Art is a gift to GOGI from GOGI student Carlos G. Smith.

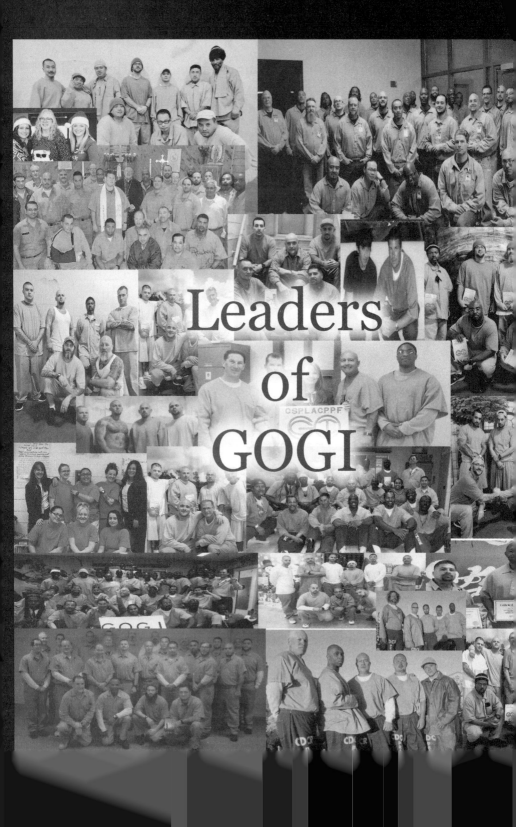

Leaders
of
GOGI

The GOGI Core Beliefs

- People are more good than bad, and bad behavior stems from poor decision making skills.

- People want to be good, successful, and want to positively contribute to society, but sometimes they don't believe they can or don't know how.

- People sometimes lack the training, examples or experience in positive decision making.

- People sometimes get frustrated and act out or resort to illegal behavior and addiction when they do not know how to make their life better through positive decisions.

- People respond well to positive and sincere reinforcement.

- People sometimes do not know how to ask for help, or if they do, they do not know how to apply the help they receive.

- People learn more from peers than from teachers, and behavior is changed more easily when peers model the desired behavior.

- People can and do develop new, productive habits, which become automatic with practice, regardless of their past or their perceived limitations.

- People's weaknesses become strengths with practice of the GOGI Tools.

- People have improved lives when they live "The GOGI Way."

The GOGI Pledge of Service

May our commitment (repeat)

To the study of GOGI (repeat)

Grant us the joy (repeat)

Of giving and receiving (repeat)

So that our inner freedom (repeat)

May be of maximum service (repeat)

To those we love (repeat)

And infinite others (repeat)

The Purpose of the GOGI Pledge of Service

A pledge is a solemn promise or undertaking. The "GOGI Pledge of Service" is a verbalized promise to use the GOGI Tools to improve our lives and the lives of others.

The "GOGI Pledge of Service" reaffirms our study and practice of the GOGI Tools, so that one day we might live our lives in constant use of the GOGI Tool, ULTIMATE FREEDOM.

The GOGI Prayer
Origin of the GOGI Prayer

Prayer and Meditation

GOGI was created by prisoners who came from every possible culture and every possible religion, or lack thereof. One of those prisoners, Mimi, just so happened to be a Christian, and she found that GOGI helped her to be a better Christian. The women in her module/pod were Agnostic, Jehova's Witness, Muslim, Buddhist and everything in between. The beauty of GOGI is that the simple Tools are a neutral, good-human place where people of all beliefs can agree. Through GOGI, the differences we perceive in each other can be diminished as we focus on our similarities.

The group of women in GOGI Campus, who created the "GOGI Pledge of Service" also created a "prayer" similar to the AA prayer, as most of the women had struggled with addiction and had attended AA meetings.

The GOGI Prayer
God, grant us the joy of giving and receiving, so our inner freedom may be of maximum service to those we love and infinite others, Amen.

Note: Mimi Jones update. After a life of jails and prisons done on the installment plan, Mimi finally got herself out of the system. She gives credit to God and GOGI. She remains clean and sober. As of this printing, she has a job in the legal field (she says, "go figure"), and her son has chosen to live with her, so she is enjoying being a mother who can be there for her child.   ♥~ *Coach Taylor*

Ultimate Freedom

GOGi

ART BY : ARMANDO SANDOVAL

Studying

GOGI

Art is a gift to GOGI from GOGI student William Granados.

—————— Chapter 22 ——————
Your GOGI Future

GOGI for Everyone
Simple Tools for positive decision making should not to be withheld from anyone, for any reason. All humans should and can have the ability to learn simple Tools for positive decision making. That is what Getting Out by Going In is doing; providing every willing human being with the GOGI Tools to increase their ability to make positive decisions.

We began our work with incarcerated men, women, and children; and, our students are now helping us expand to provide these Tools to every man, woman, and the youth, and offering an option, before they make bad decisions that result in dire consequences.

GOGI Students Living Together
For those who are in settings of confinement, ideally, individuals engaged in the study of GOGI are housed together. This concept of housing GOGI students together has proven to be the most effective approach to changing the "culture" into a positive GOGI Culture.

GOGI in Schools?
If each child was taught BOSS OF MY BRAIN, BELLY BREATHING, and FIVE SECOND LIGHTSWITCH, we would have an increased number of children smiling as they sat in overcrowded classrooms. If each child was taught POSITIVE THOUGHTS, POSITIVE WORDS, and POSITIVE ACTIONS, we would have less bullying at schools. If each and every child was taught CLAIM RESPONSIBILITY, LET GO, and FOR–GIVE, there would be fewer dropouts and fewer incidence of childhood drug use. With WHAT IF,

REALITY CHECK, and ULTIMATE FREEDOM, it is likely that we would be turning our prisons into colleges and universities because we would be drastically reducing our prisoner population.

All Children Deserve GOGI

WHAT IF we grow up as a society and admit that greed, selfishness, and harm-causing behavior never made anyone happy long term? On their death bed no individual claims that they wish they had accumulated more stuff, or wished they had climbed up the ladder squashing more people beneath them.

WHAT IF we, as a people, ensure that our children are given the educational Tools with which to create more positive decisions? WHAT IF we show them how to do this by example?

At GOGI, we believe all children deserve to have access to Tools for positive decision making which should be reinforced by peer example, in media, in schools, and at home. We also believe that prisoners and all individuals who have made poor decisions in the past deserve Tools for positive decision making so they will stop perpetuating the downward spiral within our communities.

WHAT IF we all engaged and lived our lives as an example of what is possible, not as a sorry by product of where we have gone wrong as a society? We, as a society, are only limited by the number of people who want and will work toward their own internal change. If enough individuals within the system change, the system must change to accommodate them. At GOGI, we know systemic change starts with the individual.

A Network of Positive Information

GOGI's history is rich with human effort for change. Even to this day, when a prisoner who studies GOGI is moved from one facility to another, GOGI usually goes with them, packed neatly away in their personal property. This is how the viral network of the positive GOGI Culture has resulted in tremendous expansion across the U.S.A., and throughout the world in many different languages. This is because people are the best promoters of something that is honest, something that is worth investing time to explore, and something that works.

GOGI and "Living The GOGI Way" is a positive Culture option for anyone inside or outside of prison because the word is out that GOGI Tools help everyone. GOGI and the people of GOGI are known to be honest in their effort to model a solution. The GOGI Tools are easy to apply, and everything about GOGI promotes a new and more positive lifestyle for everyone.

GOGI's expansion was participant driven. From our first workshops at the Federal Correctional Institution in Terminal Island, California, to Pelican Bay, the chain of letters started from a woman in a prison who ignited the

"Let GO The Past". Support IS Here.

THE GO WAY

No matter what part of The WORLD Your, STUDYING GOGI "YOU ARE NOT ALONE."

My signature _Jeffrey Lopez_

Print your name _Jeffrey Lopez_

spark of GOGI in a boyfriend in another state. He shared the information with dozens of his friends who studied GOGI in New York. From Arkansas to Wyoming, every state has someone sharing the simple Tools of GOGI and consequently becoming a better person and living as a good example as they emerge as a solution for their community.

Everything GOGI?

The GOGI Culture continues to grow on its own, driven by individuals who are all about making change happen. From very early on we had GOGI Cheers, GOGI Prayers, GOGI Pledges, GOGI Poems, GOGI Drawings, GOGI Talent Shows, even mothers calling their newborn a"GOGI Baby." Increasing numbers of individuals are certifying as GOGI Community Coaches to be of service to the communities they once harmed.

The Solution Emerges

From kitchen tables and the trunks of cars, the volunteers at GOGI watched otherwise discouraged and hopeless individuals in prisons and jails gain momentum in their own process of change and begin to exemplify lasting change.

GOGI encourages all students to learn and share simple Tools for choosing the positive changes they may have wanted to make, but were never quite able to follow through consistently enough to effect lasting change.

GOGI For Kids

Many of our prisoners tell us that if they were taught the GOGI Tools as children, they would not be in prison. Prevention, we believe, is the least expensive route to societal health. We tested teaching the GOGI Tools with a variety of school aged children. We even tested it with young boys in detention.

Across the board, the Tools were easily learned and easily applied by children. Keeping it simple is what GOGI is all about, for children and adults alike. And, we are relying

Art specific to COCI from COCI student Fernando Moreno

greatly on our GOGI students, who are adults, to take these Tools to the youth.

Kids "Get" It

Share GOGI with any youngsters with whom you are able to communicate. You will find they appreciate and "get" the simplicity of the GOGI Tools. Children and young adults thrive on honesty and simplicity, welcoming the practicality of learning and "Living The GOGI Way."

Less Is More

The individuals who make up the GOGI team of volunteers understand and appreciate the value of living a humble life of service. They understand the tempting trap of thinking you need the newest and best of everything. GOGI encourages all individuals who find the Tools helpful to lead by example. GOGI students practice the fine art of wanting less and sharing more.

The volunteer students at GOGI have discovered that the less they want and the less they need, the more available they are to be of service. They have also discovered that a humble life of service is the most powerful life when they use the GOGI Tool, ULTIMATE FREEDOM.

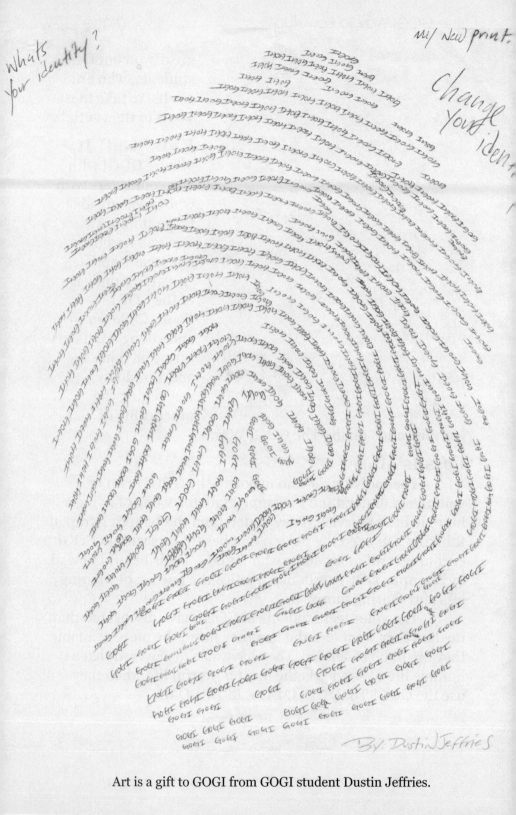

What's your identity?

My new print.

Change your identi...

Art is a gift to GOGI from GOGI student Dustin Jeffries.

Section Three

The Faces Of GOGI

Faces

of

GOGI

Getting Out
by Going In

—————— Chapter 24 ——————

The Many Faces of GOGI

Stepping Up as the Solution

Who Are the Faces of GOGI? The Faces of GOGI are those individuals who are stepping up to BE the solution needed in society today. Refusing to wait for someone else to fix what is wrong in their communities, the many individuals who are self-proclaimed as "Faces of GOGI" are from all walks of life. They are showing up as an example of service and positive decision making through their daily use of The GOGI Tools.

Individuals who are applying the GOGI Tools to their every day life realize how commonplace it is to point fingers and blame others for problems they encounter. However, armed with their GOGI Tools, these solution-minded community members are showing up as an example of the solution they once sought.

The individuals who claim to be the Faces of GOGI understand that pointing fingers is not as effective as having a positive action ready.

Having predetermined positive actions as a replacement has permitted them to move beyond the fear of change. The inherent vulnerability perceived during the change process is

Coach Taylor "emoji"
by Coach Benny G.

Art is a gift to GOGI from GOGI student Jose Rios Jiminez.

oftentimes the reason for complacency.

For me, it was the fear that I would be exposed, seen, witnessed, and possibly judged harshly by others. The last thing I ever wanted in my pre-GOGI life was to be perceived as "vulnerable."

My positive decision to volunteer inside prisons and jails gave me the courage to brave the unknown and let me feel less "vulnerable" as a result of growing strong.

What does "Vulnerable" Mean?

Just yesterday, a friend asked if it was difficult for me to be "vulnerable" in speaking from my heart, sharing the painful portions of my journey with complete strangers, and asking them to do the same.

I gave this considerable thought, as I inched forward in putting this book together, the word "vulnerable" was like a little butterfly constantly flitting in front of my face.

I knew I needed to address my perception of what it means to become, be, and remain vulnerable, as I believe my current perception of the experience of vulnerability may encourage others who are embarking on the GOGI Journey of Getting Out by Going In-ward. The GOGI journey includes placing oneself in what seems to be a vulnerable position in order to ultimately become stronger.

In the past, the word "vulnerable" caused me to think of being susceptible to something negative happening, something out of my control, and it's inevitable pain. Looking back, I believe I once felt that I needed to hide aspects of "me" or I would risk being hurt, rejected, and misunderstood.

Now, however, my life experience related to my definition of "vulnerable" is quite different.

Please Explore

Please explore with me, for a moment, a broader definition of the word "vulnerable," as I believe my current perception may offer a critical component to your own lasting internal freedom.

It could be that with a subtle perception shift, you can

more quickly identify an underlying purpose within your daily life, and thereby experience an abiding pleasure with every rising of the sun.

The many Faces of GOGI, those individuals who apply the GOGI Tools in their daily life, come to experience an expanded experience of "vulnerability," but prior to this writing, the subject of vulnerability has not been a direct discussion.

What I have witnessed, and what I have personally experienced, is all I can share with you. In the past 20 years of intense engagement with individuals embarking on their GOGI Journey to Internal Freedom, I am convinced that the current definition of "vulnerable," which is accepted across a vast majority of languages, is woefully inadequate to the potential definition of the word.

WHAT IF appearing "vulnerable" means claiming the unique power of the totality of your life experience? WHAT IF trying to "hide" or "bury" your truth is truly living in vulnerability; meanwhile, owning your thoughts, feelings, emotions and actions is the ultimate power of the human experience?

I have never known a truly strong individual who hides behind a mask. Those who hide, those who are fearful that they will become vulnerable, are, ultimately, the most vulnerable among us.

Those who are firmly planted in the truth of their choices and the truth of their life experiences may appear to the general public to be vulnerable. My experiences, however, conclude something quite different. These individuals, who stand in their truth as a vehicle of promoting good on earth are, in actuality, the strongest of us all.

With the reasoning that those who temporarily appear "vulnerable" are actually emerging as leaders-for-good, it is safe to reason that what we define as "vulnerable" is actually the gateway to our individual power, the gateway to finding a purpose-driven life, the gateway to lasting

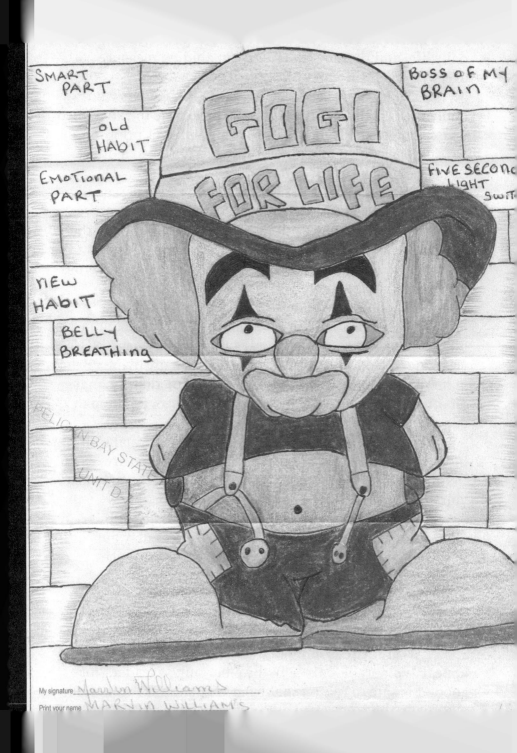

freedom.

I would propose that rather than invite individuals to be "vulnerable" we invite them to be "powerful" in their ownership of their life experience. While this may temporarily appear to be fear provoking, beyond this temporary fear is the life force power that only living in truth can provide.

A Tribe to Call Home

Humans tend to buffer the possibility of feeling vulnerable with friendships and associations they make with others. When we choose these relationships wisely, they strengthen our life's journey so we do not feel so alone.

We gather in groups, clubs, gangs, associations, careers, addictions, or a variety of other means to attempt to insulate ourselves from that which is not like "us" or uncomfortably different. At times, we may not like our definition of self, but we continue to associate with a familiar set of people, places, and things.

An affinity for the familiar does not necessarily mean distain for the different; it only means that we find comfort in that which is most like us. Aligning with these preferences we feel understood. Heard. Witnessed. Accepted. No longer out of place.

As someone who has spent a majority of my life working and associating with individuals who have very different life experiences from mine, I can tell you clearly that I am not judging anyone or anything as being better or worse. It is simply human nature to lean toward that which is familiar, even if the familiar is dangerous, destructive, and disabling.

How is it Done?

If you are not particularly fond of the results obtained by your prior associations, your prior choices, or your prior priors, how do you become a Face of GOGI and not feel like an alien in your own land? For each of us who live each day with the GOGI Tools by our side, the journey to identifying

yourself as a "Face of GOGI" is as unique as each individual. I will illustrate how it unfolded for me.

By the time my full-on adult life rolled around, I was not really all that thrilled with what I saw being played out around me by other humans claiming they were happy. It seemed to me that people were generally unhappy, mean, or clueless.

I felt isolated in a private world of intense realization that people around me were messed up, selfish, lying to themselves, addicted, insecure, and living lives that didn't seem to matter much to anyone except their own false narrative of freedom. It all seemed so shallow and so temporary. I was flustered with what was being promoted as "cool" and desirable, as well as that which was promoted as offering "freedom."

A Glimpse Fed the Fire Within

The change I desired didn't begin to happen until the bottom fell out of my life that seemed to already be at the bottom. It was at that time that I became desperate enough to be brave. Through that bravery to make different choices, I began to catch a glimpse of what "freedom" really meant.

It wasn't until some years later that I truly felt "free." The details that fill the space between the bottom of the bottom and my own internal freedom which snuck up on me a decade later, can be summed up in one word... relentless.

For me, internal freedom was a "do or die" situation. Either I was going to find a way to experience life as a happy person in the face of the unhappy people around me, or I didn't want life. Choosing the former before opting for the latter, I stopped at nothing to stuff my mind, my ears, my eyes, my hands, my heart, and my soul with every possible positive reinforcement.

I made tough choices, especially since I was living in an area where glitz and glamour defined daily life. Opting to dismiss the sex, drugs, and Rock & Roll party invitations that defined the Los Angeles area of Hollywood during that era, I chose to remain in my little apartment, as a single

Art is a gift to GOGI from GOGI student Anthony Lewis.

mother, barreling through book after book on psychology, happiness, success, leadership, religion, and spirituality.

A relentless desperation for a life purpose of any kind was at the core of my ordination as an interfaith minister, my two Masters degrees in Psychology, a doctorate degree, and the ability to gift hundreds of self-help books to local charities after absorbing ever last morsel of usable information.

All the while, I was regularly volunteering my time in prisons, engaging in soulful conversations with prisoners who seemed to be on a similar freedom quest.

Keep the Goal as Your Focus

The key to my eventual internal freedom was my willingness to feel alone in discomfort long enough to sever the ties with the old and become keenly aligned with those who had the same commitment and dogged determination. My people, places, and things changed. Eventually, how I defined myself changed, too.

It took ten years. (Don't worry, for most people it comes along more quickly, but I am a fairly slow learner.) At the ten-year mark, I could honestly say that I was a "Face of GOGI" and lived my life with the GOGI Tools helping me be the best version of me possible.

How did I know? I knew I was a Face of GOGI when every choice I made was filtered through my tools. My life became a purpose-filled journey of causing no harm and helping whenever I could. That was when I became a Face of GOGI.

Voices of the Faces

In this section of the book titled "The Faces of GOGI," you are introduced to individuals who have embarked upon the journey of Getting Out by Going In-ward for freedom. These are the Faces of GOGI. They each hope that thier own journeys will help set you free enough to embark on your journey's trajectory, should you become brave enough to embark.

Art is a gift to GOGI from a GOGI student.

The Faces of GOGI are stepping up, and standing up, and they continue to PowerUp! their communities. And, in doing so, their internal freedom is assured.

In speaking for all of us who have started and continued on this journey of internal freedom, it is our sincere wish that you, too, can look in the mirror and genuinely smile.

With this smile – the one that comes from deep within - will be an internal realization that a key that was once buried deep within you has turned and your internal freedom has been created by you to share with those on a similar path. It is at that golden moment, when you have gotten out by going inward, that you will realize, you are a Face of GOGI, too.

The GOGI Logo

The GOGI logo has significant meaning. It stands for the name, GETTING OUT BY GOING IN. You will notice that the letters G and O make the outside frame of the design. This stands for the words GETTING OUT. GOGI is about Getting Out of the prisons we create for ourselves as a result of our life experiences and responses to those experiences.

Inside the G and O, you will find a G and an I. This stands for GOING IN. At GOGI, we have learned that by GOING INSIDE ourselves, by unlocking the doors inside ourselves, we are able to find freedom regardless of where we awake each morning. We do not need physical freedom to have internal freedom. G and O (Getting Out) is only possible by the G and I (Going In). Together they provide the key to internal freedom. That is what the GOGI logo means.

The GOGI Coat of Arms

Art by Soliz

Art is a gift to GOGI from GOGI student J. Soliz.

Origin Of The GOGI Coat Of Arms

James Soliz took it upon himself to submit the GOGI Coat of Arms to help promote the concept of a GOGI family and an enduring positive culture to replace the prison or gang culture of the past. Throughout history, a Coat of Arms has represented a seal of protection, unity, and devotion. Here is what James, a true man of GOGI, says about the GOGI Coat of Arms:

This art piece is a symbol of inspiration, dedicated to all those who want change. It is a presentation of Getting Out by Going In. The breastplate symbolizes oneself getting ready to go to war with themself. Traditionally, you must look into the center of the breastplate, encountering an outer reflection. To put on the armor, we find the reflections that exist within us.

The Eagle Image Mirror exposes our underlying issues that hinder us from reaching our full potential. We can look into a mirror and like what we see, but what does the inside reflection look like? We all have a calling and after a lot of reflection, we develop a sense of an awakening of self. In the grips of the Eagle Image Mirror's claws exist two scrolls. One scroll represents a vision and the other your mission statement. The Swords represent the GOGI Tools. They are either sharp or dull. The quest is ours to determine. The lions are our guardians, symbolizing strength and courage, guiding us along the path. The vines are a true source of life, representing growth, maturity, and prosperity. The hands are a constant reminder to reach out for our goals. On top of the crown is a precious gem in the image of a heart, crafted to be worn by royalty. For where your heart is, there you will find your treasure. The T on the crown symbolizes the true self, from the breastplate up to the crown of life. Once you have elevated to this level, you have found true freedom by Getting Out by Going In. Now you can spread your wings and soar like an Eagle.

—————— Chapter 25 ——————
The **GOGI** Community of Collaboration

What is a GOGI Community?

When I volunteered at the Federal Corrections Institution at Terminal Island, in San Pedro, California, I met with prisoners each week and together we collaborated to better understand the change process. Listening to the experiences and thoughts expressed by these men is how GOGI began, and this beginning set the template for the collaboration that has defined the GOGI Culture.

In one of the earliest weekly meetings, I recall recapping our discussions by saying, "We can get out of the prisons we create in our mind by going inside for the solutions." Thus, the concept of Getting Out by Going In (GOGI) emerged. The name, "Getting Out by Going In" and the nickname "GOGI" was the first collaborative effort that would chart the future course.

Getting Out and Staying Out

When asked their opinion about getting released from prison and getting out of the system altogether, most of the men did not believe they could remain out for long because, it seemed to them, the system kept yanking them back in.

Most of the men in that group believed their situation was the system's fault, and the system needed to be fixed before they could remain free.

GOGI Pledge

May our commitment~ To the study of GOGI~ Grant us the joy~ Of giving and recieving~ So that our inner freedom~ May be of maximum service~ To those we love and infinite others.

PBSP 2017

Art is a gift to GOGI from GOGI student Sandoval.

Art is a gift to GOGI from GOGI student Rey.

Going Inside for the Freedom
Upon further exploration, however, the men agreed the problem was not going to be corrected by someone doling out money, jobs, or housing, although those things would be helpful.

The men realized the problem would only be solved if the incarcerated individual made the positive decision to "get out" of the self-imposed prisons they had created by their choices, such as their addictions, affiliations, or criminal thinking.

First, they stated, they needed to go inside themselves to create the freedom from within.

The Name Fit
The name Getting Out by Going In and "GOGI" seemed to fit this emerging discussion of positive life changes because the conversation always seemed to come back around to the individual.

As we collaborated on various aspects of individual choice, an informal "Culture" began to form, with other men within the prison wanting to join our weekly group discussions.

100 Men on the Floor
It did not take long for our first group of six or eight members to expand incrementally until, at one point, we had more than 100 men gathered in the gym. It was quite a sight. One hundred men on their backs, on the floor of the gym, putting one hand on their chest and one hand on their belly as we explored the newly-created tool called BELLY BREATHING.

Collaboration Works
The collaboration with the men in our smaller weekly group paved the way for the larger workshops, as the emerging GOGI leaders "recruited" their friends to join in on the discussion that was "GOGI," before any of us knew what that meant.

Art is a gift to GOGI from GOGI student Candace Gray.

Art is a gift to GOGI from GOGI student Erickson.

Grassroots GOGI

As a "listening" organization, the non-profit organization of GOGI was birthed from these conversations. And, truth be told, it was the effort to raise money to make paper copies of handouts that drove me to seek non-profit status.

When one of our leaders was transferred to a federal institution in Taft, California, he wanted to take his GOGI with him. I figured that if others were to be transferred, they might want their GOGI, too.

Sensing a continued growth to support what was unfolding, a non-profit organization seemed to be the only viable support system that would permit sufficient autonomy to let the prisoners find the answers for themselves.

The fundraising to get enough money to send printed pages to a GOGI Leader in a prison several hundred miles from this Home GOGI Group was the first time the collaboration included community members.

Collaborating on Tools

Each of the GOGI Tools was created through a collaborative effort within a small community of individuals intensely engaged in the quest for internal freedom. And, in the development of these tools, the motivation to share them was immediate.

The first six tools were developed by the men at Terminal Island. The second group of tools was developed by the women of GOGI Campus at the Los Angeles County Jail.

The First Tool

The first GOGI Tool emerged from a conversation during a Peer Mentor Circle meeting. One man stated, "What you are saying, Coach Taylor, is that I need to be the boss of my brain." And with that statement, the first GOGI Tool got its name. BOSS OF YOUR BRAIN is, even today, one of the most popular, and certainly one of the most fundamental of the GOGI Tools.

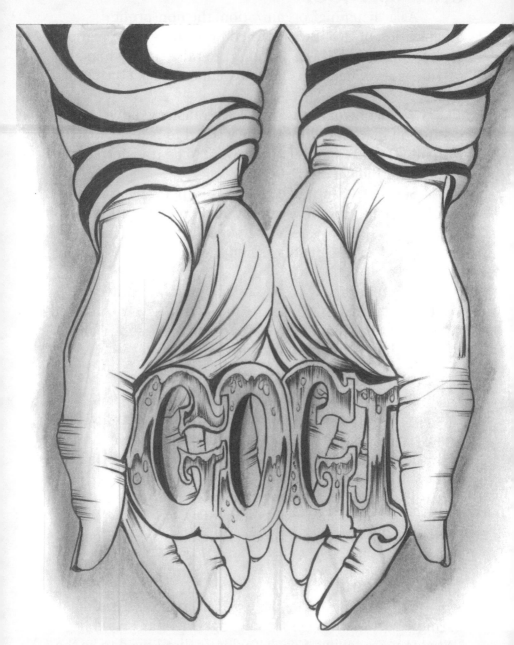

Art is a gift to GOGI from GOGI student Gen Kan.

The Tool Order

In this ongoing collaboration which is GOGI, even the order of the Tools has been modified. I remember a Veteran approaching me and stating that there was no way he would tell a group of Veterans that they should LET GO before they knew the tool BOSS OF YOUR BRAIN. As a result of that conversation, the order in which we presented the Tools was modified.

The GOGI Calendar of Study

Even the GOGI Calendar of Study was a collaboration of student input. One student hoped he would not always study his GOGI alone. Another group of men came up with the idea of a study calendar so that no one would ever feel alone on their GOGI Journey.

While developing the GOGI Calendar of Study, one student stated that since the Mayan Calendar was ending, it was only fitting that a GOGI Calendar is offered to the world. And yet another student sat with the mathematical aspect of the calendar and made certain each Tool was represented equally across all months of the year.

The Importance of Flexibility

In supporting the building of positive decision making muscles, it is essential to remain flexible, as growth is rarely linear. In my own experience, I have found that remaining open to new ideas, or new applications of the Tools has widened my own perspective of their use and importance.

What I have learned about flexibility is this; the more I use my GOGI Tools the more forgiving and understanding I become. The more I use my GOGI Tools the more empowered I am to see beyond weaknesses, to the buried strength below the surface. The more I use by GOGI Tools, it seems the fewer irritating things happen throughout the day. GOGI is an elegant collaboration of all humanity, realizing each individual's perspective has value and can be considered.

What We Know

What I have come to know, and what the ardent student of the GOGI Tools comes to understand as well, is that freedom of choice can lead humans toward the experience of an internal prison, or one of internal freedom.

To the extent that the individual chooses life-affirming actions, they incrementally experience a more pleasant feeling than those times when they make choices that are inherently destructive to self or others. Making positive choices leads to positive experience which leads to positive interactions, which leads to positive results. In all honesty, it does not happen all that quickly at first, but positive does generate more positive... even if it takes a little time.

Similarly, negative choices usually fly under the radar for a while. They, all of a sudden, they come slamming down on you in a big way. Negative choices lead to more negative choices.

The Beauty of it All

The beauty of it all is in the simplicity of the formula. Positive leads to more positive. Negative leads to more negative.

When combined with GOGI's simplified Tools for positive decision making, there is every chance in the world that anyone can embark upon the journey toward internal freedom.

Inevitable Expansion

While the number of individuals engaged in the informal study and daily use of GOGI Tools continues to grow, the organization of GOGI remains committed to its original vision of relying on the students as the solution. Our model of success is dependent upon community members to realize their power to effect change. Empowering community members with the Tools needed to make the most positive decisions has been the ultimate collaboration.

Empowered with the GOGI Tools, and united in

HARPER II

service of their communities, the students of GOGI are emerging as the solution they once sought to find. Their commitment to living in service is behind the continued expansion of the GOGI Culture.

Positive Byproduct

As a positive byproduct of GOGI's reliance on the students to create and promote the versatility of the Tools, a belief in the unlimited potential of the human has emerged. This belieft in human potential is a core philosophy of all GOGI studies.

An individual who is aligned with utilizing their GOGI Tools in their daily life will undoubtedly speak of their unlimited potential. Even when things seem down, they rarely get too far down for the students of GOGI.

Universality of GOGI

What remains quite remarkable to this day is the universal nature of GOGI, and the applicability for all individuals to use of the GOGI Tools. When GOGI began to be the "topic on the yard," and an increasing number of individuals signed up on the "program" list, it was interesting to see the wide range of types of individuals who found the GOGI Tools helpful.

Enemies and Friends

It is not uncommon to see otherwise enemies sitting in a PowerUp! Peer Mentor Circle discussing the tool of the week, as if they had been best friends all their lives. It was with great joy that I experienced the women embracing the concepts of GOGI with equal fervor to their male counterparts. And the greatest joy of all was in witnessing school children grab on to the Tools as if it were an ice cream cone on a hot summer day.

The universal nature of GOGI is what solidifies my knowledge that the GOGI Culture is here to stay. I have often told my students that 300 years after my passing, it is likely that the GOGI Culture will still be around. And, I believe this to be true. It is too simple, too elegant, and too

Art is a gift to GOGI from GOGI student David O.

needed to not find its way into the backbone of the human experience. But what does that mean to those who have strong religious beliefs or convictions? What does GOGI mean for their life experience?

What About Religion and God?

The positive thing about most religions and most spiritual beliefs is that, at their core, they teach similar concepts of being a good person. There are GOGI students from every religion, culture, and spiritual belief. Students of every possible belief system find the GOGI Tools to be helpful in strengthening their ability to be a better person. The strength of GOGI can be found in the student's deep respect for the human condition, the human nature, and the human's unique life experience. Grace is what makes a GOGI student a solution within their community. The GOGI Student lives gracefully among those who appear to be different.

Students of GOGI tend to believe the individual forms concepts of a God or an omnipotent universe or some otherworldly power based on experiences and exposure to cultural norms.

GOGI students will often reflect that their fellow students are really "not all that different" once they start discussing their GOGI Tools.

They may have a different accent, or religion, or skin color, but once they start speaking their GOGI, the similarities are at the forefront of the conversation.

Supporting Others

As an organization, GOGI supports the belief that each human has the right to believe as they choose. We find it is productive when the universal language of The GOGI Tools enable that choice to be supported in others, as well.

What's Next?

You may be asking, "What's next?" That is a question to consider when you have downtime and can let your mind

Art is a gift to GOGI from GOGI student Keith Erickson.

Art is a gift to GOGI from GOGI student Victor Ojeda.

wander a bit. Much of what GOGI emerges to become is going to be directly related to the collaborations established when our students start stepping up as the solutions in our communities.

GOGI has expanded to include indivdiuals from all walks of life. It is quite frequently I am asked if GOGI could work for kids, or parents, or police, or politicians. My response is always the same, expressing my sincere belief that the GOGI Tools are for all mankind. Anyone who is able to make a decision can improve their life experience with the application of these simple tools.

Your Imagination is your Limit

What is next for the expansion of the GOGI Culture and Living the GOGI Way? The answer to that question is yours. What I know is the future is only limited by your ability to imagine beyond the immediate, and consider new possibilities.

In the absence of your imagination, you may be leaving your fate and the fate of those you love, in the hands of someone else. Armed, however, with your GOGI Tools, you are able to construct a life of which you can be proud.

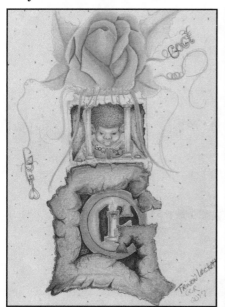

Art is a gift to GOGI from GOGI student Javier Garcia, Jr.

The Faces of GOGI Graduates

Your Face Belongs Here!

Chapter 26

The Faces of The Solution

Each individual has the ability to create a meaningful life. I witnessed this in the lives of thousands of GOGI students who rose out of the ashes of their self-imposed fire. These individuals came to shine the light of hope created by the GOGI Tools to others who remained buried in the rubble of their choices.

No other remedy worked quite as effectively to salvage a drug-destroyed, or gang-limiting life than to have that individual witness the change they sought played out in the life of another. The "problem" emerged as an example of the "solution" for which they were desperately seeking.

To better understand a solution for my own life, I first needed to take a look at my problems. Until I was willing to look at the problem (me and my perspective), the solution (me and future choices) was not apparent. With nearly two decades of the GOGI Journey behind me, I can say with confidence that the solution is consistently buried just beneath the surface of the problem.

A few years ago, and prompted by grant funding for the non-profit organization Getting Out by Going In, we started tracking the student completions of GOGI's softbound courses. The data spanned a period of 1,000 days. We documented more than 27,000 completions across 40 prisons during that time period. The following pages contain a list of the men and women who completed eight or more of those courses, thereby qualifying them as a "GOGI Superstar."

There are many thousands of students not represented in this data, but each and every individual engaged in the sincere practice of Living the GOGI Way is preparing themselves to PowerUP! their community – by, and through, their example.

The GOGI Superstars

GOGI Superstars are those registered students with documented completion of 20 units of college-level GOGI course study.

ABEL OLIVO
ABEL ROSAS
ADALBERTO GOMEZ
ADAM HENDERSON
ADOLFO BERMUDEZ
ADRIAN GURROLA
AHMAAD SIMS
ALAN GRIFFITH
ALBERT FRANCO
ALBERT VELEZ
ALBERTO BARRETO
ALBERTO GUERRERO
ALBERTO TOLENTO
ALEJANDRO CENTENO
ALEJANDRO FERNANDEZ
ALEJANDRO MACHUCA
ALEJANDRO SANDOVAL
ALEJANDRO SANTANA
ALEX JAE
ALEXANDER VALENTINE
ALFONSO CASTILLO
ALFONSO GARCIA
ALFRED SANDOVAL
ALFREDO VALENZUELA
ALLEN ADAMS
ALLEN FONG
ALLEN GOODEN
ANASTACIO RAMIREZ
ANDRE CENICEROS
ANDRE PULIDO
ANDREI BECERRA
ANDREW GALLEGOS

ANDREW LINCOLN
ANDREW LOPEZ
ANDREW MCCARTER
ANDREW SALAS
ANDREW THOMPSON
ANDREW TILLMAN
ANDREW TOA
ANDREW VASQUEZ
ANDREW VELEZ
ANGEE BURRELL
ANGEL BALDERRAMA,
ANGEL RAMIREZ
ANGEL RUELAS
ANGEL VALENCIA
ANTHONY ANTILIA
ANTHONY CABRERA
ANTHONY CHAMBERS
ANTHONY DEAN
ANTHONY FLORES
ANTHONY GRIFFITH
ANTHONY LOPES
ANTHONY OROPEZA
ANTHONY SPALDING
ANTUNEZ ALEXANDER
ARMANDO LOPEZ
ARMANDO MACIEL
ARMANDO QUINTANILLA
ARMANDO VILLALOBOS
ARNOLDO COSIO
ARTHUR BATES
ARTHUR NEVAREZ
ARTHUR RAMIREZ

ARTURO BENTANCOURT
ASHISH LAL
AURA YESINIA AMAYA
BAILEY GONZALEZ
BENITO ARROYO
BENITO LORENZO
BERNARDINO RENTERIA
BERRY DENTON
BILLY MORALES
BINH NGUYEN
BOBBY THOMAS
BOBBY WHITE
BRAD MILLER
BRANDON BRANSCOMBE
BRANDON FLEEMAN
BRANDON HEIN
BRANDON POWELL
BRANDON VILLALOBOS

BRETT BOHART
BRIAN SMART
BRIANT LOCKETT
BRINT CLARK
BURTON HEBROCK
CALVIN SMITH
CAMERON MITCHELL
CARLOS GARCIA SMITH
CARLOS LUGO
CARLOS OCHOA
CARLOS ORTIZ
CARLOS SANABRIA
CARLOS SANCHEZ
CESAR CAMACHO
CHAD DIAS
CHAD WILBURN
CHANH MINH DANG
CHARLES CLARK

MY GOGI WAY — TONY MORENO

Before GOGI I had no spark,
And my thinking was always dark.
These tools my mind ignited
And here and I found many people who felt just like I did.
Together we studied and formed this class
Forming some friendships that would forever last.
Our positive thoughts became words then actions
By learning Boss Of My Brain and 5 Second Lightswitch.
Today I claim responsibility and practice belly breathing
As my reality check becomes my ultimate freedom.

The GOGI Superstars

GOGI Superstars are those registered students with documented completion of 20 units of college-level GOGI course study.

CHARLES GOODWIN
CHARLES RITCHIE
CHHAILEE REY
CHRIS LAMB
CHRISTIAN BERCIAN
CHRISTIAN BORDA
CHRISTIAN MEDRANO
CHRISTOPHER BARKLEY
CHRISTOPHER BRADFORD
CHRISTOPHER BURLEW
CHRISTOPHER D. OERDING
C. HENDRICKSON
CHRISTOPHER JAGERSON
CHRISTOPHER JONES
CHRISTOPHER LOA
CHRISTOPHER MUNJE
CHRISTOPHER RIGSBY
CHRISTOPHER RIVERA
CHRISTOPHER SANTANA
CHRISTOPHER SUCCAW
CLARENCE HARVEY
CLARENCE REESE
CLEOPHUS FITTS
CODY RANDAZZLE
CONDA HILL
CUONG NGUYEN
CURTIS MEEKS
CURTIS WILSON
DANIEL COBARRUBIAS
DANIEL GUFFEY
DANIEL LOYD
DANIEL OROZCO

DANTE FULTON
DARA YIN
DARIUS MILLER
DARREN BARBER
DARRYL BACA
DAVID CUMMINGS
DAVID DAWSON
DAVID DONOVAN
DAVID FAGAN
DAVID GONZALES
DAVID HERNANDEZ
DAVID HOPE
DAVID LOPEZ
DAVID MORENO
DAVID NANEZ
DAVID SANCHEZ
DAVID SAUCEDO
DAYVAUGHN WILLIAMS
DEL EDDY COLEGROVE
DELBERT HULSEMAN
DEMETRIUS JENKINS
DENNIS GRIMSTEAD
DENNIS THIES
DEREK ROBINSON
DEREK SIDA
DIEGO HUERTA
DOMINGO GONZALES
DOMINGO VARGAS
DOMINIC JUGE
DONALD BRADISH
DONALD SIMPSON
DOUGLAS JORDAN

DOUGLAS LUNSFORD
DRAKE WALKER
DUSTIN JEFFRIES
DUSTIN MINOR
DUSTIN STANFORD
DWAYNE LUCAS
EDDIE NAPOLES
EDDIE NEVAREZ
EDWARD FURNACE
EDWARD HARRIS
EDWARD SANDERS
EFRAIN GARCIA
EFREN BECERRA,
EIEZER PRADO
ELIAS SANCHEZ,
ELOY RUBALCABA
ELVIS ARMANDO TUCK
EMIGDIO VALDEZ

EMILEANNO CROSS
ERIC BOUNVONGXAY
ERIC CASTILLEJA
ERIC ROBLES
ERIC ZAMORA
ERICK FABIAN
ERICK RODRIGUEZ
ERICK SCOTT
ERNESTO BERNAL
ERNESTO OCHOA
ERNESTO PEREZ
ERNESTO RODRIGUEZ
ERNESTO SERRANO
ESEQUIEL CONTRERAS
EVAN GAINER
FABIAN MENDOZA
FAUSTO MINOR
FELIPE SANDOVAL

These Tools are Worth it
A gift to GOGI by CA SVSP GOGI Leader Jacob Taele

I am definitely striving to change,
The first thing I had to do was be the BOSS OF MY BRAIN.
BELLY BREATHING wasn't easy for me to learn at all,
Especially when I've been breathing wrong for so long,
I'm proud to say 'I did it' now I'm fully committed,
To The GOGI Way of living and FIVE SECOND LIGHTSWITCHES,
Which is in my best interest, and I mean that with a passion,
I went from negativity to POSITIVE THOUGHTS, WORDS, and ACTIONS.
I CLAIM RESPONSIBILITY for all of my decisions,
From my time on the streets, to my time now in prison,
Today I LET GO of the small things and the big things,
Who would've thought my entire life, GOGI is what was missing?
I know how to FOR–GIVE, because I am safe from harm,
WHAT IF I am not my past? WHAT IF I don't create alarm?
My REALITY CHECK is this: I know I'm not perfect.
But if the ten and two rule leads to ULTIMATE FREEDOM,
Then learning these tools are worth it.

The GOGI Superstars

GOGI Superstars are those registered students with documented completion of 20 units of college-level GOGI course study.

FERNANDO ECHEGARAY
FERNANDO MORENO
FERNANDO OROZCO
FERNANDO PEREZ
FIDEL PEREZ
FORTINO LOPEZ
FRANCISCO BARAJAS
FRANCISCO BRISENO
FRANCISCO FERNANDEZ
FRANCISCO GUTIERREZ
FRANCISCO LOPEZ
FRANCISCO VASQUEZ
FRANCISCO VILLARRUEL
FRANK BURNETT
FRANK ORTA
FRED BROWN
FRED HUANTE
FROYLAN RODRIGUEZ
GABINO SANDOVAL
GABRIEL CASTILLO
GABRIEL DELGADO
GABRIEL SINGER
GABRIEL VINCENT RUIZ
GARLON ROBINSON
GARY GALLION
GARY SELLERS
GEORGE BRISTOL
GERALD WADE
GERVEY CONTRERAS
GIANNI VAN
GILBERT ACOSTA
GILBERT ESCOBEDO

GILBERT QUIROZ
GILBERTO GARCIA
GLENN MASON
GONZALO BARBOSA-
SALGADO
GONZALO GONZALES
GONZALO NAVARRO
GREGORY RECTOR
GUY NELSON
HECTOR RUIZ
HENDRIX MONTECASTRO
HENRY ZARAZU
HERIBERTO GUTIERREZ
HERMAN ROBINSON
HO NGUYEN
HORACIO LEDON
HUAN NGUYEN
HUGO GOMEZ
HUGO PINEDA
HUNG VIET VU
IAN SHAYNE DUNCAN
ISAAC DELGADO
ISIDRO SANCHEZ
ISMAEL CONTRERAS
ISMAEL VALDIVIA
IVAN CESAR MOSQUEDA
IVAN RAMIREZ
JACOB HUTCHINS
JACOB STEELE
JACOB TAELE
JAIME VALENZUELA
JAIRES PEREZ

JAMES BRIGGS
JAMES CROWTHER
JAMES CURTIS
JAMES DUNCAN
JAMES FAGONE
JAMES HIGGINBOTHAM
JAMES HOWARD
JAMES MILLIKEN
JAMES RELEFORD
JAMES SCHANROCK
JAMES SERNA
JAMIE PALACIOS
J. RICHARDSON
JARED YAFFE
JARRED VIKTOR
JASON BROWN
JASON EDMON
JASON PEREZ

JASON YATES
JAVIER DELATORRE
JEFF STEIN
JEFFERY GARCIA
JEFFERY YOUNG
JEFFREY LAMONT
JEFFREY LANTZ
JEFFREY MCKILLIGAN
JEFFREY PANTALEON
JEFFREY RICKS
JEFFREY THOMPSON
JEFFREY WARD
JEFFREY WEAVER
JERALD HOLMAN
JEREMY BINION
JEREMY C. TIONGSON
JEREMY HARRISON
JEROME GOLDEN

WHAT IF? By Coach Kori Darty

WHAT IF I embrace my future from my past experiences, and
LET GO of what I have no control of?
WHAT IF the things that hurt the worst, really help the most?
WHAT IF the people I don't like have a piece to my puzzle?
WHAT IF I am quick to listen, and slow to speak?
WHAT IF I am my own enemy?
WHAT IF I am careful on which battles I choose to fight?
WHAT IF I learn how to learn?
WHAT IF I am honest, that I am afraid; that I am alone?
WHAT IF there's a purpose for my pain?
WHAT IF my trials are relay my testimonies for a greater good?
WHAT IF my purpose and gift is to give the world a lift?

The GOGI Superstars

GOGI Superstars are those registered students with documented completion of 20 units of college-level GOGI course study.

JESSE CASTANEDA
JESSIE HURTADO
JESUS BORJAS
JESUS PADILLA
JESUS PLATA LOPEZ
JESUS TORRES
JESUS VARGAS ALCALA
JESUS ZAVALA
JIMIE TRAN
JOAQUIN MARTINEZ
JOAQUIN MENDIETTA
JOE HERNANDEZ
JOEL CASTILLO
JOEY CARRILLO
JOEY TYLER
JOHN BLACKWOOD
JOHN GILLOGLEY
JOHN HARPER
JOHN LOYD
JOHN PARK
JOHN REMSEN
JOHN SOTO
JOHNNY HOWE
JOHNNY LEWIS
JOHNNY PEREZ
JON HOUSTON
JONATHON HAAS
JORGE USTRELL
JOSE AGUILERA
JOSE AMADOR
JOSE CAPACETE
JOSE CARLOS RODRIGUEZ

JOSE CERVANTES
JOSE DELPALACIO
JOSE FLORES
JOSE HERNANDEZ
JOSE HERNANDEZ
JOSE MALANCHE
JOSE MARTINEZ
JOSE MIGUEL
JOSE MOSQUEDA
JOSE PEREZ
JOSE QUINONEZ
JOSE RODRIGUEZ
JOSEPH BRACAMONTE
JOSEPH JOHNSON
JOSEPH JONES
JOSEPH KEEL
JOSEPH LOPEZ
JOSEPH ROUSE
JOSUE OROZCO
JOSUE SANCHEZ
JUAN CORONA
JUAN GARCIA
JUAN HATCH
JUAN HERRATE
JUAN HUARACHA
JUAN MIGUEL ELLINGBERG
JUAN MOLINA
JUAN SUAREZ
JUAN ZUNIGA
JUANITO PURUGGANAN
JUDE MERAZ

JUSTIN FLICKINGER
JUSTIN JAMES ALLEE
JUSTIN MONTGOMERY
KATHY SNOOK
KEATON STEPHENS
KEITH ERICKSON
KEITH SHERMAN
KELLY ELLIS LUND
KENNETH AZLIN
KENNETH BARKSDALE
KENNETH BENJAMIN
KENNETH BROWN
KENNETH SINGLETON
KEVAUGHN HARRIS
KEVIN KEPFORD
KEVIN LEWIS
KEVIN M. SCHMIDT
KEVIN ROSE

KEVION LYMAN
KIRK RIVERS
KIRK STAPLETON
KORY DARTY
KRISTIAN EDGAR MONTOYA
KUNLYNA TAUCH
KURT GOODSON
LACHAPELLE CHENDA
LANCE BRITTAIN
LAVONTAHE BROWN
LAWRENCE ALEXANDER
LEONARD HOBSON
LEONARD SNIDER
LOUIE CHAVEZ
LOUIS HALL
LOVELLE CHAPMAN
LUIS ANGEL CORELLA

The GOGI version of Me,
is what I love to be.
Leave the negative where it lay,
get away, rehabilitate in new ways,
BOSS OF MY BRAIN from the inside out,
positivity and insight will sprout.
Want to give a shout, to the Coaches
who GOGI, all out.
GOGI for life, no more doubt,
so internalize the tools and live well,
even inside a prison cell.

My signature _Kirk Rivers_
Print your name _KIRK RIVERS_

The GOGI Superstars

GOGI Superstars are those registered students with documented completion of 20 units of college-level GOGI course study.

LUIS BUSTAMANTE	MATTHEW TURNER
LUIS GUTIERREZ	MAURICE AINSWORTH
LUIS PINEDA	MAURICE RAYBON
LUIS RAMIREZ	MAURICIO AYALA
LUIS ROBLES	MELVIN BURKS
LUIS SALAZAR	MELVIN DAVIS
LUIS SILVA	MELVIN SMITH
LUPE MARTINEZ	MICHAEL A. ALTAMIRANO
LUSVIN CARDONA	MICHAEL ALMEDA
MALCOLM COLEMAN	MICHAEL ARTEAGA
MALIGI TUITASI	MICHAEL EHLOW
MANUEL CALDERON	MICHAEL F. PEREZ
MANUEL HERNANDEZ	MICHAEL FICKLIN
MANUEL JIMENEZ	MICHAEL GARZA
MANUEL SILVEIRA	MICHAEL GRAMATA
MARIA FIERRO	MICHAEL SPENCER
MARCO ORDONEZ	MIGUEL GUILLEN
MARCOS SANTISTEVAN	MIGUEL PAREDES
MARIO ARCIGA	MIGUEL RUIZ-FIGUEROA
MARIO LOPEZ	MIGUEL SAENZPARDO
MARIO PADILLA	MIGUEL WHITE
MARKISE DAVIS	MILLARD BAKER
MARLON MELENDEZ	MOISES GARCIA
MARTIN SANCHEZ	MOISES TEJEDA
MARTIN SANTANA	NATEEL SHARMA
MARTIN TALAVERA	NATHANIEL BARRETT
MATTHEW BARNES	NATHANIEL MARTIN
MATTHEW FOCKAERT	NHUT VO
MATTHEW MULLEN	NICKOLAS SALCIDO
MATTHEW PAWLOWICZ	NICKOLAS VEGA
MATTHEW POOLEY	NOE LOPEZ
MATTHEW SHEPHARD	NOE ROJAS

NORMAN MILES	PEDRO AYON
OMAR RIGO RAMIREZ	PEDRO AYON-GANDARILLA
OSCAR DIAZ	PERRY STUART
OSCAR RUIZ	PETER EDELBACHER
OSVALDO GARCIA	PETER SANTISTEVEN
OSVALDO SOLIS	PETER SIGMUND,
OUHAN CHEN	PETER SOTO
PASQUAL CAMPOS	PETER ZAMORA
PATRICK GRIFFIN	PHILIP LOZANO
PATRICK KIRK	PHILLIP DELGADO
PATRICK LEACH	PHILLIP KENNEDY
PATRICK MEJIA	PHILLIP MALDONADO
PATRICK SANTOS	RAFAEL FIGUEROA
PAUL CAIN	RAKAYLON LYONS
PAUL GARCIA	RAMIRO RUIZ
PAUL LATANZIO	RAMON MENDOZA
PAUL LEWIS	RAMON REYES
PAUL SANCHEZ	RAMON ZAPATA,

STOP!

FOCUS ON THE SMART PART OF YOUR BRAIN.

TAKE BACK THE POWER!

FOR YEARS AND DECADES, I SUFFERED FROM THE RUNAWAY BRAIN SYNDROME. I WASN'T IN CONTROL OF MYSELF. SO MANY THINGS INFLUENCED ME IN DIFFERENT DIRECTIONS, AND EVER SINCE I COULD REMEMBER, I DID WHAT PEOPLE TOLD ME TO DO. I WAS ALWAYS THE FLUNKY IN MY LITTLE CROWD. MY EMOTIONAL PART AND OLD HABIT PART WERE IN FULL CONTROL OF MY BRAIN. I COULD NEVER SAY NO; MY EMOTIONS WOULDN'T LET ME. AND IT BECAME HABITUAL, FROM CHILDHOOD INTO ADULTHOOD. MY BRAIN RAN RAMPANT, DRAGGING ME ALONG. IT WASN'T UNTIL I ENCOUNTERED GOGI THAT I WAS ABLE TO BECOME THE BOSS OF MY BRAIN ONCE AND FOR ALL. NOW I ACTUALLY FEEL FREER THAN I DID ON THE STREET, STRANGE AS IT SOUNDS, THAT IT WASN'T UNTIL I CAME TO PRISON THAT I ULTIMATELY BECAME FREE!

EVA CONTRERAZ
GOGI BOOK STUDY STUDENT

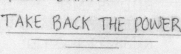

The GOGI Superstars

GOGI Superstars are those registered students with documented completion of 20 units of college-level GOGI course study. .

RAUL MARTINEZ
RAVINESH SINGH
RAYMOND DILLON
RAYMOND SABEL
RAYMOND TEQUIDA
RICARDO MOCTEZUMA
RICARDO VEYNA
RICHARD AGUIRRE
RICHARD BIGHOUSE
RICHARD BOYDE
RICHARD FISO
RICHARD GUERRERO
RICHARD HERNANDEZ
RICHARD HOLGUIN
RICHARD HOWARD
RICHARD HURTADO
RICHARD JACKSON
RICHARD JARAMILLO
RICHARD MAQUINALES
RICHARD MILEY
RICHARD NEWMAN
RICHARD OCHOA
RICHARD SALAZAR
RICHARD TOVAR
RICHARD WYATT
RICK CHRISTIANSEN
RICKEY HUERTA
RITO ORTEGA
RIVELINO LOPEZ
ROBBIE RIVA
ROBERT BALDASARO
ROBERT BARNES

ROBERT BECERRA
ROBERT CHURCH
ROBERT DOMINGUEZ
ROBERT GOMEZ
ROBERT IMES
ROBERT LOPEZ
ROBERT MINA
ROBERT PRICE
ROBERT QUIROZ
ROBERT ROJAS
ROBERT SANDOVAL
ROBERT STEINER
ROBERT STEWART
ROBERT VASQUEZ
RODERICK JOHNSON
RODGER ALLEY
RODNEY BECKER
RODNEY PATRICK MCNEAL
RODNEY UTLEY
RONALD KENNEDY
RONNIE JOHNSON
ROSS WATERBURY
RUBEN CORTEZ
RUBEN GARCIA
RUBEN OLASCOAGA
RUBEN TAJIMAROA
RUDY LIMON
RUDY RAMOS
RUENDY VILLALOBOS
RUSSELL BAXTER
RUSSELL BUCHANAN
RYAN CARL

RYAN OLSEN
RYAN TURNER
SALVADOR HERNANDEZ
SALVADOR LUNA
SALVADOR MORALES
SALVADOR NEGRETE
SALVATORE MAGGIO
SAMBAN CHENG
SAMUEL BERGARA
SAMUEL CAEZ
SAMUEL DIXON
SANDIE SUMALPONG
SANTIAGO ESTRADA
SAUL CAMPOS
SAVON DAVIS
SCOTT DOWNEN
SCOTT LUNNY
SCOTT TAYLOR

SELSO CASTANEDA
SERGIO CEDILLO
SERGIO MIRANDA
SEVIN OBRAYANT
SHARDISE MALAGA
SHAWN CHANEY
SHAWN MCMILLAN
SHAYLOR WATSON
SHEB ISBELL
SILUS VALSON
SINH NGUYEN
SIONE FAKALATA
SIRILO ALVAREZ
SKYLER CHARLIE
SON LORN
SOPHEAK CHHANG
SOPHEAP CHHEANG
SORIYAA EK

Whether you go through this life as a menacing raucous Animal, or a self loathing, anti-social agonizing human being,
The application of these tools shall transform you into the person you strive on being,
With these tools you shall, tame the Angry Beast within you, that is the cause of pain,
You shall be equipped with the strength to climb out of Depths of Despair,
even find shelter from the pessimistic Rain,
you will chisel away at the old stone of self and create a new form,
Just as a catapillar goes through Metamorphasis
So shall you take a new form and thus be Reborn.

My signature _____Sandoval_____ ID number _____ Location __P.V.S.P__
Print your name __Joseph A. Sandoval__

The GOGI Superstars

GOGI Superstars are those registered students with documented completion of 20 units of college-level GOGI course study.

STEPHEN PRICHARD
STEVE ALLEN ESPINOZA
STEVEN BURKHOLDER
STEVEN DESHAZO
STEVEN GONZALES
STEVEN GREEN
STEVEN HARPER
STEVEN OSMENT
STEVEN ZINDA
STEVIE COLLEY
STEVIE THOMAS
SUNNY NGUYEN
TARAN DOWNING
TERAUCHI GOLSTON
TERENCE WORD
TERRANCE LAUSHAUL
THAE SOTEAR CHOUN
THOMAS BAUGH
THOMAS NELSON
THOMAS SHELTON
THOMAS VIGIL
THUE VANG
TIMOTHY STALEY
TINO PESE
TOMAS ROMERO
TOMAS SORTO
TOMMY BROWN
TONY MORALES
TONY OTTO BROWN
TRACY PAUL
TRAVION WILLIAMS
TRAVIS REAY

TRAVON SIMMONS
TRESHAWN TREJO
TROY MCDONALD
TROY SYKES
TRUONG NGUYEN
URIEL RODRIGUEZ
VICTOR CARRASQUILLO
VICTOR DEALBA
VICTOR DEANDA
VICTOR MORALES
VICTOR NAVA
VICTOR OJEDA
VICTOR ROBLERO
VICTOR VERA
VINCENT J. VIGIL
VINCENT MEDRANO
VINCENT MORRIS
VIRGIL CLARKE
WALTER FOSTER
WALTER VILLANUEVA
WESLEY SOLIS
WILLIAM BECKER
WILLIAM FERNANDEZ
WILLIAM HOPEAU
WILLIAM OATHOUT
WILLIAM SUMPTER
WILLIE HINES
WOODY HARTMAN
XIA LIN
YOURY GOMEZ
ZENON FLORES

A Note About Section Four

Section One
In Section One of this book, you learned about the GOGI Tools.

Section Two
In Section Two of this book, you learned about The GOGI Way and it's applications, now and in the future.

Section Three
In Section Three of this book, you met The Many Faces of GOGI who helped develop the GOGI Tools and demonstrated their ability to effect positive change.

Section Four
In Section Four, you have the ability to practice all that you have learned, while supporting others who wish to "power up" their life experience, too. This is because Section Four of this book contains The PowerUp! Community Meeting Manual. This Manual empowers the user with all the Tools needed to inspire change within their community and within themselves. Section Four provides all that is needed to make simple, lasting Tools available to anyone who seeks simple solutions that can be applied to create lasting positive change.

Section Four

PowerUp!

Community Meeting Manual

PowerUp! Community Meeting Manual
Table of Contents

Part One

PowerUp!
Let's Get Started

I. The Basics of **PowerUp!**

What are PowerUp! Community Meetings?

PowerUp! Community Meetings are positive weekly gatherings of individuals formed in Peer Mentor Circles to reinforce use of the GOGI Tools. These meetings are ideal for those who wish to contribute to a positive community engaged in the practice of the GOGI Tools.

What are the GOGI Tools?

The GOGI Tools are simple ways any individual can get, or remain, on course for creating their optimal life. These Tools were developed from the most effective and proven psychological strategies for behavioral change, fused with practices from all religions and cultures for optimizing goals and personal satisfaction in life.

Why is it called PowerUp!

PowerUp! is a statement of the purpose of the meetings. Participants are encouraged to "power up" and become a solution within their communities to seemingly difficult situations or circumstances through their skill in utilizing The GOGI Tools.

What is a Peer Mentor Circle?

A Peer Mentor Circle is no more than 12 participants who are members of a closed circle. When there are 13 potential members, two Peer Mentor Circles are formed. PowerUp! Peer Mentor Circles have no more than 12 members.

Who is Authorized to Facilitate PowerUp!?

A Facilitator of PowerUp! may be an experienced group leader or instructor well-versed in all aspects of The GOGI Tools as well as The PowerUp! Manual.

NOTE: *Any individual with sufficient formal GOGI training, such as a Certified GOGI Community Coach, is an ideal Facilitator of all aspects of PowerUp! as well as other GOGI educational options.*

Why is GOGI Material Needed?

While this Manual provides you with the format and structure of PowerUp! Meetings, without adequate knowledge, experience or materials, your success may be limited.

Rights to Use of Materials:

GOGI reserves the right to disallow use, or refuse access to, and/or limit or refuse reproduction of the PowerUp! Community Meeting Manual when it is not utilized according to the outlined purpose and protocol provided herein.

Stay Connected

Community Members are encouraged to engage and remain informed as GOGI continues to grow and expand in services such as advanced certifications, correspondence study, group study, eLearning, and others. Updates of the manual are offered as free downloadable files.

Additional information is available on the GOGI website at www.GettingOutByGoingIn.com or by contacting:
GOGI Headquarters
P.O. Box 88969
Los Angeles, CA 90009

II. An Introduction to **PowerUp!**
By Coach Taylor, GOGI Founder

Imagine a world where children and teenagers are taught GOGI Tools with which they can make positive decisions. Imagine adults who model these Tools in their daily choices, making it simple for children to create meaningful and purpose-driven lives. Imagine a universal language of internal freedom shared by all cultures, a language that unites rather than divides.

This is the world I have witnessed unfolding along my journey as the founder and first volunteer for the non-profit organization Getting Out By Going In (GOGI). I have seen children being taught The GOGI Tools by their incarcerated parents. I have seen these parents on telephone calls and during family visits teach the Tools, because they are determined to chart a path very different for their offspring than the one they created in the absence of Tools.

I have seen incarcerated adults modeling what it is like to live an internally free life. I have enjoyed seeing community members coming to realize that if someone emerging out of prison can live an internally free life, then it would be reasonable to assume just about anyone else could live that way, too.

I Have Witnessed

I have witnessed in dozens, if not hundreds, of instances, rival gang members and former enemies gather in GOGI Peer Mentor Circles to share the GOGI Tools in the safe and supportive environment of our PowerUp!. I have seen color lines, along with all other exclusionary criteria, otherwise defining who is a friend and who is not, disappear when the focus is on being of service to community, The GOGI Way.

The world I would like you to imagine is not some

far off dream, it is the world in which I live every day of my life. I witness these things inside some of the most notorious prisons, and this is why PowerUp! Community Meetings were created by our GOGI students. PowerUp! permits this powerfully positive way of living to find a home within the heart of all humans, giving all humans the format, the permission, and even the excuse to be magnificent.

In this Section of the Book

In this section, you will find all the details you will need to hold your very own PowerUp! Community Support Meetings.

These meetings are the vision of our GOGI students who know that when united in a common language of positive decision-making, there is nothing a community is unable to accomplish. In a very real way, there are few problems the GOGI Tools can't help redefine as an opportunity.

PowerUp! Emerges

PowerUp! as a format for the study of GOGI emerged from the need to find the solution within the very thing defined as the problem. PowerUp! offers you permission to get out of our own way and unite in one great cause of identifying and living a purposeful life path.

GOGI at the Bay

In 2015 and 2016, Getting Out by Going In received grant funding to provide "programming" to prisoners locked in the highest security housing units of Pelican Bay State Prison and California Corrections Institution, both of which were within the State of California Department of Corrections and Rehabilitation. Going from one cell to the next, I convinced maximum security prisoners to simply "look" at the GOGI material, even if they did not normally program. I shared with them that GOGI was created by and for prisoners, and I had traveled a great distance to be there, so they would be doing me a favor to give it a glance. Month after month I would return, distributing more and more courses as word spread throughout the housing unit that GOGI was the real deal.

After several months of service, I came to know a few of the names, and many of the faces of men who had not seen the light of day for 10, 20 and sometimes 30 years. Actually, in thinking about it, I was probably the first non-officer, non-chaplain, "real" person some of those men had seen since they were in the courtroom waiving goodbye to their families. You don't think of those things at the time, but, I guess it was a new experience for all of us.

Once the concept of GOGI caught on, I would hear one prisoner giving a warning to cells down the hall. "GOGI's in the house, you better have your course work ready." The men would holler this out, notifying the others that a GOGI representative had been permitted into the unit.

I remember one time I made it into the housing unit without the normal fanfare. I walked into the housing unit of CCI on A or B yards with my officer escort. I made my way quietly to one of the cells where a very enthusiastic GOGI student was housed. Upon my approach, I heard him speaking. I wondered if he had purchased a smuggled cellphone and I hoped I was not going to be walking up to a situation I did not want to see. I stood back a few feet and listened.

Curiosity

Curiosity eventually forced my approach. There he was on the top bunk with his mouth as close to the air vent as possible. He was talking about GOGI, but was single-celled and had no one else in the cell. I went to the adjacent cell. Sure enough, the guy next door was in the same position. These two men were actually talking about GOGI.

"Are you two men holding a GOGI meeting," I asked, as I approached his cell door.

"Damn, Coach Taylor, you can't walk up on people like that," came his reply.

"Yeah, sorry about that, but I was hearing some GOGI talk and couldn't resist."

As it turns out, since the men were not permitted to be out of their cells at the same time due to their security level, they formed their very own meetings through the air vents to PowerUp! their ability to make positive decisions. And they were not alone.

At Pelican Bay State Prison, it was not uncommon for one of the men in a unit to hold a PowerUp! Meeting loud enough for the men in adjacent cells to chime in with their own contributions. At the Bay, the housing configurations were modular in format, but the cell bars made open discussions possible. While seated on their two-inch mattresses, men in their cells reviewed their materials and conducted very organized and well-documented meetings.

Once these higher security prisoners were transitioned to less restrictive housing, they continued with their GOGI meetings, inviting others to join in this new culture and new way of navigating life on the open prison yard.

Graveyard GOGI

One night, I was permitted to visit a jail where the only time they could do GOGI studies was on the graveyard shift, as there was an officer there who was supportive of rehabilitation, even if it could only happen at 9:00 at night. We called it Graveyard GOGI.

I arrived at the jail during a snow storm, and pushed the buzzer and was let into a very dark hallway to another buzzer that led me to an elevator. When the door opened, a voice on the intercom instructed me where to go to find the officer.

Ultimately, I was led past hundreds of sleeping bodies in darkened dorm-like housing to a door. When it opened, the light was so bright I needed to squint. Inside the room, nearly 100 men in brightly colored jail uniforms were assembled in a neatly-formed circle. Their leader, Coach Tevita, led them in the GOGI Pledge of Service followed by an activity that highlighted their knowledge and use of the tools.

Meetings of like-minded individuals were driven by the student's eagerness to share and explore the application of the GOGI Tools. Rare was it to find someone who did not want to speak about, share, and exemplify the tools.

GOGI students tried, tested, and explored the optimal way to empower communities for good. Through their contributions and refinement of details, the PowerUp! Community Meeting format is now available for anyone.

The GOGI Calendar

The GOGI Calendar unites all GOGI studies and reinforces the power that comes when an entire community is focused on something positive at the same time. Even Graveyard GOGI was united in the study of the same GOGI Tool as all other students of GOGI had as their focus.

The Four Sets of Tools

There are four sets of GOGI tools:
TOOLS OF THE BODY
TOOLS OF CHOICE
TOOLS OF MOVING FORWARD
TOOLS OF CREATION

The GOGI Tools

Within each set are three specific Tools. Each Tool was created to address a need that had been unmet by traditional programs or efforts for change. Each Tool, however, is consistent with proven strategies for success. The difference is, with PowerUp!, the most complex operations of the body and brain are simplified for easy use.

The PowerUp! Community

The PowerUp! Community includes anyone who wants to show up as a solution for their community, realizing that in living a life of service their internal freedom is a natural by-product.

III. The GOGI Tools

Tools of The Body
BOSS OF MY BRAIN

BELLY BREATHING

FIVE SECOND LIGHTSWITCH

Tools of Choice
POSITIVE THOUGHTS

POSITIVE WORDS

POSITIVE ACTIONS

Tools of Moving Forward
CLAIM RESPONSIBILITY

LET GO

FOR–GIVE

Tools of Creation
WHAT IF

REALITY CHECK

ULTIMATE FREEDOM

IV. **PowerUp!** Your Community
From Coach Taylor, GOGI Founder

An Invitation to PowerUp!
With a high demand for GOGI Tools to be offered to all mankind, it was imperative to find a way to offer the GOGI Tools to anyone who believes that access could help them make better decisions.

The PowerUp! Community Meetings include anyone and everyone into the wonderful world of GOGI.

Excitingly, this manual includes all the information necessary to facilitate PowerUp! Community Meetings.

PowerUp! Community Meetings were created to meet demand for a free and open source way to share GOGI studies. PowerUp! provides a solution because it is an attendance only, ongoing support meeting for both new and seasoned GOGI students.

Join me in Living the Vision
When I state that I live the vision of unity each day, I truly mean that I live the vision of a united humanity every day. This is a vision brought to reality by society's perceived problems who finally realized they were society's only real solution.

I hope you catch the vision of all that PowerUp! can mean to humanity. I certainly wish that what I see regularly will become a commonplace occurrence for all mankind. It's time we PowerUp! as a people.

What is PowerUp!?
As the "Culture" of GOGI people engaged in applying the GOGI Tools to their daily lives began to evolve, it became a simple solution to what was perceived to be a

pretty big problem of chronic poor decision making. This caused a great demand for GOGI materials.

To this day, it is a real challenge to provide all those seeking materials and support for their stated needs. GOGI students asked for a simple way Certified GOGI Community Coaches could share their knowledge with the world.

As a result, PowerUp! Community Meetings were created. In this section of the book, you will be provided all the information you need to facilitate PowerUp! Community Meetings.

Getting Started

Know that this material is all you need to hold your PowerUp! Community Meetings, but access to the GOGI books and courses increase successes of participants.

Where to Start

For a new PowerUp! Meeting, always start with The Team Building Meeting. The Team Building Meeting is repeated after every 15 meetings to ensure protocols and procedures do not deviate over time.

Authorized Credit

Participants should be made aware that the GOGI non-profit organization will not track attendance nor issue credit for PowerUp! Meetings. If the facility or school is willing to issue credit, it must be titled "PowerUp!"or "PowerUp! Community Meeting."

PowerUp! Community Meetings are ongoing and not intended as a formal program with an end date. The authorized program name is "PowerUp!" and not "GOGI." The only approved full title for the program is "PowerUp! Community Meetings."

While no certificates will be issued by GOGI Headquarters for attending PowerUp! Meetings, an institution or organization may issue attendance-based credit, providing the credit is worded in exactly the following manner: "PowerUp! Community Meeting Attendance" or "PowerUp!." No other title of credit is authorized.

Mandatory Peer Mentor Circles

Conduct all PowerUp! Meetings in Peer Mentor Circles of 5-12 participants. This is absolutely mandatory, as Peer Mentor Circles of 5-12 participants define the PowerUp! Meeting.

For example, in one large gym, up to 120 students could assemble in 10 Peer Mentor Circles for weekly meetings. Many circles may exist in the same room as space permits, but all participants will sit in closed Peer Mentor Circles of 5-12 members.

Failure to meet in this manner waives the permission for authorized use of PowerUp! or the GOGI Tool names and materials.

Official GOGI Materials

PowerUp! Community Meetings and all other GOGI studies are more effective when students are provided GOGI materials and courses. PowerUp! Community Meetings were created as a very basic introduction to GOGI and an ongoing support meeting that can exist only with handouts as materials for participants.

It is understood that lasting learning occurs most effectively with supportive GOGI materials. To order official GOGI materials contact: info@gettingoutbygoingin.org.

Local Credit

Remember: GOGI Headquarters neither tracks nor issues credits for PowerUp!, which are attendance-based support meetings. GOGI Headquarters only issues credit and certificates for completion of our softbound course workbooks and our coaching programs. Credits, if provided, are issued locally, by the hosting organization.

Meeting Facilitator Requirements

GOGI authorizes PowerUp! to be facilitated by GOGI Coaches or other GOGI Authorized Facilitators. Meetings that are permitted by an institution, school or hosting organization are intended to provide participants with an ongoing support meeting format for GOGI Tool study.

Permission to Deliver PowerUp! in a "Programming" Format

Permission is granted to offer PowerUp! as an official "program" whenever the institution or organization includes no fewer than one Certified GOGI Community Coach or Authorized Facilitator for every 11 other participants, and each participant receives copies of the weekly handouts.

Meeting Length, Frequency, Leadership

Powerup! Meetings are most effective when they are 90-120 minutes in length, held weekly, in the required Peer Mentor Circle format, and facilitated by a GOGI Community Coach.

Stay on Calendar

Coordinate all PowerUp! Meetings with the GOGI Calendar of Study. The GOGI Tools are always studied by calendar, not in a step manner. As such, no make-up meetings are needed or permitted. PowerUp! is an ongoing support meeting with tools repeated throughout the year. Do not worry about attendees "missing" a tool if a weekly meeting is missed.

Power Up! Round

The PowerUp! Round is 15 meetings in length. In these 15 weekly meetings, group members will participate in one Team Building Meeting, 12 Tool Meetings according to the Calendar of Study, one Recap Meeting and one Celebrate Success Meeting. These 15 meetings complete one round of PowerUp!

PowerUp! Cycle

The PowerUp! Cycle of Study is 30 meetings. This means that participants will attend two Team Building Meetings, 24 Tool Meetings, Two Recap Meetings, and Two Celebrate Success Meetings. Of course, we suggest ongoing attendance that is continual support, but in those cases where rotation of participants is required, each student should be permitted to complete no less than one full PowerUp! Cycle. When asked how long PowerUp! lasts, students may accurately reply that PowerUp! is a support meeting that should not end. For those who must have an end date, a full PowerUp! Cycle of 30 meetings would be the minimum program duration.

The PowerUp! Team Building Meeting

The Team Building Meeting begins a 15-week round and will be repeated after every 15 meetings.

The PowerUp! GOGI Tool Meetings

After the Team Building Meeting, 12 consecutive meetings are held according to the GOGI Calendar of Study.

The PowerUp! Tool Review Meeting

After the Team Building and 12 consecutive Tool Meetings, the Peer Mentor Circles hold the Tool Recap Review.

The PowerUp! Celebrate Success Meeting

After the Tool Recap Review Meeting, participants Celebrate Success. Because of the ongoing nature of PowerUp!, this meeting does not celebrate completion; but provides an opportunity for participants to focus on and share improvements and achievements, and real life experiences with the Tools.

PowerUp! and the GOGI Calendar of Study

PowerUp! and all GOGI independent, small group, online, leadership, group studies, and Coach Certification Programs worldwide are coordinated to the GOGI Calendar of Study. The GOGI week begins on a Monday.

The first Monday of each month determines the weekly Tool, which is the Tool studied all week. Where there is a 5th Monday, all Tools for that month are reviewed.

GOGI Pledge of Service to Community

PowerUp! Meetings always conclude with the GOGI Pledge of Service to Community, which reminds all participants of their ability to be an example of a solution to challenges within their communities.

May our commitment (repeat)

To the study of GOGI (repeat)

Grant us the joy (repeat)

Of giving and receiving (repeat)

So that our inner freedom (repeat)

May be of maximum service (repeat)

To those we love (repeat)

And infinite others (repeat)

Why a Pledge Of Service?

All students of GOGI unite with our GOGI Pledge of Service. This pledge defines our purpose and is repeated at the end of every PowerUp! Community Meeting. Remaining in Peer Mentor Circles, each group will rotate leading the pledge for the larger group.

V. Peer Mentor Circle Goals

- **BOSS OF MY BRAIN** - Do Peer Mentor Circle Members understand SMART PART, EMOTIONAL PART, and OLD HABIT PART?

- **BELLY BREATHING** - Can Peer Mentor Circle Members identify where their breathing is most focused by placing one hand on their chest and one on their belly?

- **FIVE SECOND LIGHTSWITCH** - Can Peer Mentor Circle Members identify alternative thoughts and actions which are available to replace automatic thinking?

- **POSITIVE THOUGHTS** - Can Peer Mentor Circle Members identify the THREE P's?

- **POSITIVE WORDS** - Do Peer Mentor Circle Members know the THREE P's?

- **POSITIVE ACTIONS** - Do Peer Mentor Circle Members know the THREE P's?

- **CLAIM RESPONSIBILITY** - Do Peer Mentor Circle Members realize that the GOGI Tool is concerned with their actions today?

- **LET GO** - Can Peer Mentor Circle Members practice the physical act of HAND - SQUASH - TOSS, and practice it on small annoyances?

- **FOR–GIVE** - Do Peer Mentor Circle Members understand that FOR–GIVE is related to safety from harm, not forgiveness?

- **WHAT IF** - Can Peer Mentor Circle Members declare positive outcomes related to positive choices?

- **REALITY CHECK** - Can Peer Mentor Circle Members understand that failure does not eliminate prior successes?

- **ULTIMATE FREEDOM** - Do Peer Mentor Circle Members act on and understand the concept of living in service of others?

VI. GOGI Calendar of Study

The GOGI week starts on a Monday. Where there is a 5th Monday in the month, review all tools

JANUARY
Week 1 BOSS OF MY BRAIN

Week 2 BELLY BREATHING

Week 3 FIVE SECOND LIGHTSWITCH

Week 4 POSITIVE THOUGHTS

FEBRUARY
Week 1 POSITIVE WORDS

Week 2 POSITIVE ACTIONS

Week 3 CLAIM RESPONSIBILITY

Week 4 LET GO

MARCH
Week 1 FOR--GIVE

Week 2 WHAT IF

Week 3 REALITY CHECK

Week 4 ULTIMATE FREEDOM

APRIL
Week 1 BOSS OF MY BRAIN

Week 2 BELLY BREATHING

Week 3 FIVE SECOND LIGHTSWITCH

Week 4 POSITIVE THOUGHTS

MAY
Week 1 POSITIVE WORDS

Week 2 POSITIVE ACTIONS

Week 3 CLAIM RESPONSIBILITY

Week 4 LET GO

JUNE
Week 1 FOR--GIVE

Week 2 WHAT IF

Week 3 REALITY CHECK

Week 4 ULTIMATE FREEDOM

JULY
Week 1 BOSS OF MY BRAIN

Week 2 BELLY BREATHING

Week 3 FIVE SECOND LIGHTSWITCH

Week 4 POSITIVE THOUGHTS

AUGUST
Week 1 POSITIVE WORDS

Week 2 POSITIVE ACTIONS

Week 3 CLAIM RESPONSIBILITY

Week 4 LET GO

SEPTEMBER
Week 1 FOR--GIVE

Week 2 WHAT IF

Week 3 REALITY CHECK

Week 4 ULTIMATE FREEDOM

OCTOBER
Week 1 BOSS OF MY BRAIN

Week 2 BELLY BREATHING

Week 3 FIVE SECOND LIGHTSWITCH

Week 4 POSITIVE THOUGHTS

NOVEMBER
Week 1 POSITIVE WORDS

Week 2 POSITIVE ACTIONS

Week 3 CLAIM RESPONSIBILITY

Week 4 LET GO

DECEMBER
Week 1 FOR--GIVE

Week 2 WHAT IF

Week 3 REALITY CHECK

Week 4 ULTIMATE FREEDOM

VII. The Four Sets of GOGI Tools ... and Their Functions

TOOLS OF THE BODY
The GOGI Tools of the Body empower you to take control of how you act and react to life's inevitable challenges and opportunities with: **BOSS OF MY BRAIN, BELLY BREATHING, FIVE SECOND LIGHTSWITCH.**

TOOLS OF CHOICE
The GOGI Tools of Choice put you in control of your thoughts, your words and your actions with a simple filter you can use to create opportunities and avoid obstacles: **POSITIVE THOUGHTS, POSITIVE WORDS, POSITIVE ACTIONS.**

TOOLS OF MOVING FORWARD
The GOGI Tools of Moving Forward let you move beyond your past as you turn your challenges into your opportunities: **CLAIM RESPONSIBILITY, LET GO, FOR-GIVE.**

TOOLS OF CREATION
The GOGI Tools of Creation permit you to design your life in a way that brings you lasting joy, contentment, meaning, and purpose: **WHAT IF, REALITY CHECK, ULTIMATE FREEDOM.**

Living The GOGI Way
When an individual utilizes these simple tools in their everyday life, they often claim they are "Living The GOGI Way." Regardless of religion, country, culture, language, size, shape, or other factors, many students of The GOGI Way state they are "GOGI 4 Life," meaning they will endeavor to use their tools long after they have learned the function and applicability. The GOGI Tools are a gift to all mankind from individuals who have been harmed, and those who have caused the greatest harm to others. This is their proposed solution for all mankind. Students of the GOGI Tools often agree that all mankind may experience the contentment that results from living a life of service, which is the focus of all GOGI studies.

Part Two

PowerUp!

Peer Mentor Circle Guide
and
HANDOUTS

PowerUp! Community Meeting

PowerUp!

Team Building Meeting

Start any new PowerUp! group with this meeting and repeat this meeting every 15 meetings.

This PowerUp! Team Building Meeting is the first meeting for new Peer Mentor Circles and is also to be held after the completion of 15 meetings. The Team Building Meeting is informative and administrative, and reviews meeting details, as well as GOGI history, purpose, and mission. PowerUp! is intended as an ongoing community meeting for new and experienced GOGI students. While all Tool related meetings are held according to the GOGI Calendar of Study, this Team Building Meeting is always held after completion of 15 meetings regardless of the GOGI Calendar of Study.

Call your PowerUp! Team Building Meeting to Order

(Read Aloud)

"We call our PowerUp! Team Building Meeting to order. Our PowerUp! Meetings are all community meetings to reinforce our use of the GOGI Tools. The GOGI Tools were created by and for students of GOGI to share simple strategies for increasing success in life. PowerUp! permits us to create positive community experiences through the sharing of the GOGI Tools when studied according to our GOGI Calendar of Study. PowerUp! Meetings are for anyone, regardless of their knowledge or use of the GOGI Tools."

Why Do We Have a Calendar of Study?
(Volunteer To Read)
"All PowerUp! Meetings and GOGI Studies are coordinated with the GOGI Calendar of Study. We do this with respect to one of the first GOGI students who was in a prison isolation cell. He wrote a letter to GOGI and stated that he hoped one day he would not study his GOGI Tools alone. All PowerUp! and GOGI studies are coordinated to the GOGI Calendar of Study, so no one will ever feel alone in their study of the GOGI Tools."

The PowerUp! Purpose
(Another Volunteer To Read)
"The purpose of our PowerUp! is to support the use of The GOGI Tools in a community meeting format."

Peer Mentor Circles
(To Be Read Aloud)
"All PowerUp! Community Meetings are conducted in Peer Mentor Circles of 5-12 participants. If we are not in our circles yet, now is the time for us to form PowerUp! Peer Mentor Circles. Where possible, we remove desks, tables, and other obstacles in the way of tightly formed peer circles of 5-12 participants for the meeting."

Coach Taylor's Invitation to PowerUp!
(GOGI Coach or Peer Mentor To Be Read Aloud)

"From GOGI founder and lead volunteer, Coach Taylor

Dear PowerUp! Participants,
In 2002, a small group of prisoners and I sat on the cool tile floor of the gym/chapel of FCI Terminal Island in San Pedro, California. Each week we discussed possible solutions to life's challenges and explored simple ways these challenges could be overcome. In our time together, I took notes and would return the following week with

information from my studies as a psychology student. Out of these conversations, GOGI was born; a positive culture of decision making tools created by those who needed them the most. GOGI is an ever-growing group of solution-minded community members just like you. GOGI students are choosing to use GOGI Tools to help them make the most positive decisions possible. GOGI students state that living life "The GOGI Way" has enabled them to emerge as a solution for their families and communities.

I have witnessed with my own eyes as the GOGI Tools became a viable solution for tens of thousands of individuals seeking ways to overcome life's inevitable challenges. These PowerUp! Community Meetings were created to make certain you have the opportunity to study the GOGI Tools. While GOGI was once delivered only in a "program" format where a course was to be completed, PowerUp! permits you to study GOGI as a way of life, not simply as a program. PowerUp! also permits you to share GOGI with family and friends. PowerUp! is designed to be taken to the streets by people just like you and offered as a viable alternative to poor decision making.

PowerUp! emerged when the students of GOGI could no longer sit back and let their peers languish on long waiting lists to get into a "program" for GOGI studies. The students of GOGI requested and assisted in the development of PowerUp! as a solution. GOGI has come a long way since 2002, when the first GOGI students were sitting in a small Peer Mentor Circle tossing around the idea that to "get out" of prison one might need to "go inside" their own mind for the answers.

As you can imagine, it was not an easy journey to get GOGI to the place where PowerUp! is now being suggested beyond the walls of prison for all school children to learn.

The GOGI Tools, created by prisoners and for prisoners, evolved as a solution for all mankind, having emerged from the darkest places on earth to shine the bright light of possibilities for us all.

PowerUp! releases GOGI to the street and as a PowerUp! participant, this is your personal invitation to join the solution. My hope is that you learn and use your GOGI Tools and that you find value in choosing to live your life "The GOGI Way" by making every decision matter, because it does.

With Love,

Coach Taylor
GOGI Volunteer

Group Comment Time
Participants are encouraged to discuss Coach Taylor's letter.

Participate in PowerUp! Check-in
(Volunteer To Read)
"Each member of a Peer Mentor Circle is invited to briefly state their name, reflect on the most positive thing that occurred during the week, and mention GOGI Tools that were applicable, or declare their intended outcome of their PowerUp! participation."

Peer Mentor Circle Guidelines
(Another Volunteer To Read)
"We now review, revise, or determine our Peer Mentor Circle group name and our guidelines. For example, "confidentiality" and "no cross talking" are common guidelines."

In your group documentation write down:
• Your Group Name: "Peer Mentor Circle Group Name"
• Please create three to five group guidelines.
• Participants write down names of group members.
(Note: If there are more than 12 members, break into two different Peer Mentor Circles).

Peer Coach Howe's Letter (Read Aloud)
A Message from Coach Johnny Howe

The entire GOGI Community knows you can make an impact in your community with the GOGI Tools. We all have our stories of our journey through life, but let me just share a few words leading up to my volunteerism with GOGI and how I came to be asked to write this welcome letter.

I began serving my life sentence in prison in 1990. Back then, I was stubborn and resisted anything that might have helped me. I was denied parole a few times and continued to not take responsibility for my life. In truth, I was in a mental and physical prison. And then, through a series of events—including meeting the lead volunteer of GOGI, Coach Taylor—I slowly started to listen.

The GOGI Tools changed my life because in becoming part of the solution, I suddenly had a purpose. With GOGI, I learned the decision-making tools I was never taught growing up. These Tools would have helped me want to- and actually believe I could- achieve something more for myself.

In 2010, after my first GOGI course completion, I was invited to "change the culture of prison" as a certified GOGI Coach. Part of my training included facilitating Peer Mentor Circle groups and helping other people learn the GOGI Tools. In being of service, I began to experience true freedom, even though I was still incarcerated.

In leading or participating in PowerUp!, you will be given an opportunity to feel a sense of community and hope, to re-build relationships with family that were once destroyed, and to give addicts and violent people the chance to pick up a GOGI Tool—instead of a drug or weapon.

I can tell you now that after 28 years, I am finally on the outside. What we as incarcerated and formerly incarcerated can offer by sharing the GOGI Tools and living "The GOGI Way" will not only prepare incarcerated men and women to handle life behind bars, but help everyone to be better prepared for when they are released; they will have Tools to cope with life in the real world.

From my own experience as a free man, I can tell you the GOGI Tools, like REALITY CHECK, help me as I figure out how to manage my finances for the first time in my life—food is expensive out here! BOSS OF MY BRAIN helps me deal with the crazy Los Angeles traffic, and the insanity of Costco market's parking lot. ULTIMATE FREEDOM reminds me of the most important lesson I've learned—that being of service to others as a GOGI Coach and licensed drug and alcohol counselor is what truly keeps me free. I wish you well on your journey to freedom, and on your journey as a GOGI PowerUp! Community Meeting participant. I know that as you participate in PowerUp!, you are going to help change so many lives, and some of you won't even know the impact right away.

I sincerely hope to meet you out here someday, so we can continue helping prisoners, their families, and other members of the community as they are released from their own personal prisons, whether they are actually made of concrete and barbed wire or only in their minds. Thank you for your help. It's nice to have you as part of the solution.

Coach

Johnny Howe

GOGI 4 Life, Coach Johnny Howe
Behind bars for 28 years | Mentally free as of 2010
Physically free as of February 13, 2018

Group Comment Time

Discuss Coach Johnny's letter.

Common PowerUp! Questions FAQs
(Volunteer To Read.)

"Regardless of your level of GOGI knowledge, every 15 weeks we review the frequently asked questions during our Team Building Meeting to keep the information fresh in our minds and make certain our meetings remain purely "PowerUp!". We will have one volunteer read each of the below numbered paragraphs. Participants may review other information later."

(Volunteers to read the following paragraphs aloud: Paragraphs 1, 2, 4, 8, 9, 11, 12 and 15. All others are informational in nature)

#1   What is GOGI anyway?
Getting Out By Going In (GOGI) is a non-profit organization dedicated to empowering individuals to increase their positive decisions by using easy to understand decision making Tools.

#2   Is PowerUp! the same as GOGI?
PowerUp! is the introduction to the GOGI Tools and ongoing support meeting, which requires no text or study materials and is attendance-based. PowerUp! is simply the attendance-based support meeting. If credit is provided for PowerUp!, it will be generated by the hosting organization, not by GOGI.

#3   Can I be in GOGI Leadership Training and attend PowerUp!?
Yes, you can be engaged in the formal GOGI certificate programs or coach certification studies and attend PowerUp! Meetings. PowerUp! Meetings support GOGI studies. PowerUp! Meetings are not designed to replace formal course study.

#4   How does PowerUp! Help Me Learn GOGI?
PowerUp! Meetings reinforce the GOGI Tools in a community of like-minded participants. This helps, alot.

#5   Who started GOGI?
GOGI was created in 2002 when Founder, Coach Taylor, began volunteering at a United States Federal Prison in San Pedro, California. The men and, eventually, women and incarcerated youth who contributed to GOGI from 2002 until 2009, developed all aspects of the GOGI Tools now available through PowerUp!.

#6   When and Where are Meetings held?
PowerUp! Meetings are facilitated by GOGI Coaches, or Authorized Facilitators and may be held anywhere at any time and usually dependent upon facility or hosting organization availability or permissions. *(By the way, PowerUp! is a meeting appropriate for school children, church groups, civic organization and the general public, too!)*

#7   Does PowerUp! Cost Anything?
PowerUp! is a free, open-source meeting to promote the understanding and use of the GOGI Tools. No organization may solicit outside funding for themselves in order to provide PowerUp! at a cost to participants or cost to any population. No participant should be charged or taxed to participate. If costs are inevitable, such as meeting space, it is the participants' opportunity to find donated space and volunteerism. PowerUp! is a volunteer-run, community supported, open-source meeting to support GOGI Tool learning.

#8   Is Attendance Credit Given for PowerUp!?
If you are attending a PowerUp! Meeting inside a school or institution, it is likely your attendance is being tracked. They might even provide attendance credit of some sort. PowerUp! is a way to introduce GOGI and is not the same as formal GOGI Courses.

#9   Why GOGI and Why PowerUp!?

Why GOGI? Because the Tools are simple. Why PowerUp!? Because the positive change is fun to share with others.

#10   Who benefits from attending PowerUp!?

People who attend PowerUp! and who study the GOGI Tools come from all walks of life, all careers, all levels of education, all cultures, all religions, all races, all sizes, all shapes and all colors. And, in most cases, they heard from a like-minded peer that using GOGI Tools helped create new possibilities for their life.

#11   How Do I Use the Tools?

Choose to be determined to establish the tool of the week in your mind and body as the automatic way you handle things. This will enable you to pull this Tool out of your GOGI Toolbox when it is most needed. Eventually, you won't even have to think about it. Because of your practice, it becomes a habit you do automatically. We repeat the Tools to create a positive habit.

#12   Which Tool is Best for Me?

Nearly everyone who uses the GOGI Tools says they have a favorite Tool they use more than others. They tell their friends they know all the Tools, but they have their favorite Tool they use for every situation possible. The fact is, all you need is one Tool. GOGI students tell their peers that with one Tool, you will have all the power you need to move beyond people, places, things and choices that no longer benefit you.

#13   What does Living "The GOGI Way" Mean?

The idea of living your life "The GOGI Way" means nothing more than including simple decision-making tools to your decision making process. Being skilled at making positive decisions will help you become the solution.

#14   Repeat, Repeat, Repeat.

The key to lasting change and improvement in anything is practice and repetition. GOGI students call this repetition "GOGI 4 Life." They find that the Tools become second nature after a while.

#15   What is the Purpose of PowerUp!?

The primary purpose of Power Up! is to provide the GOGI Tools to anyone and everyone who may have an interest.

#16   Taking PowerUp! to the Streets

PowerUp! permits participants the opportunity to take the GOGI Tools to the streets and share them with others.

With the completion of the FAQs, we continue with the meeting.

PowerUp! Participant Check Out

Each participant is invited to complete one of the following:

1) This week I will...
2) My favorite part of the meeting was...

Close your Meeting

(To Be Read Aloud by Coach or Peer Coach)

"We have completed this Team Building Meeting. Now is the time for us to close this PowerUp!. The next twelve meetings will be tool related and will follow our GOGI Calendar of Study. As always, we close this meeting with our GOGI Pledge of Service to Community, which invites us to become a positive solution for others. All students of GOGI are encouraged to memorize our pledge of service. Please repeat after me:"

May our commitment (repeat)
To the study of GOGI (repeat)
Grant us the joy (repeat)
Of giving and receiving (repeat)
So that our inner freedom (repeat)
May be of maximum service (repeat)
To those we love (repeat)
And infinite others (repeat)

PowerUp! Community Meeting
PowerUp!
BOSS OF MY BRAIN
Hold This Meeting:
First Week of Jan., April, July, Oct.

Remember: PowerUp! Meetings may be held any day of the week as long as they are held according to the GOGI Calendar of Study which begins on Monday. If there is a fifth Monday in the month, tools studied that month are to be reviewed. All tools are repeated four times each year. Therefore, there is no such thing as a "make up" or "catching up" or doing two tools in one week when a previous meeting is missed. The community of GOGI remains on calendar for all meetings, thereby uniting all studies everywhere.

Administrative Duties and Details
If there are announcements, administrative details, voting, or distribution of materials, these tasks are to be conducted before your meeting begins. (All peer mentor groups should be formed after admin duties and details.)

Peer Mentor Circles
(Read Aloud)
"PowerUp! and all GOGI studies are defined by our GOGI Calendar of Study and our Peer Mentor Circles. If we have not already done so, at this time we break from the larger group meeting into our Peer Mentor Circles of 5-12 participants."

Start Your Meeting
(Volunteer To Read Aloud In Peer Mentor Circles)
"The GOGI Tools are studied worldwide according to the
GOGI Calendar of Study. We unite with others according
to this schedule, so no one will feel they are alone in
their effort to make positive decisions. We believe in
everyone's ability to benefit from this positive community
of individuals united on the GOGI Calendar of Study.
Therefore, we call this PowerUp! BOSS OF MY BRAIN
Meeting to order, and we join in the Tool being studied by
students of GOGI everywhere."

Review of the Tools
(A Volunteer Recites Or Reads The GOGI Tools.)

BOSS OF MY BRAIN
BELLY BREATHING
FIVE SECOND LIGHTSWITCH
POSITIVE THOUGHTS
POSITIVE WORDS
POSITIVE ACTIONS
CLAIM RESPONSIBILITY
LET GO
FOR-GIVE
WHAT IF
REALITY CHECK
ULTIMATE FREEDOM

The PowerUp! Purpose
(Volunteer To Read)
"The objective of PowerUp! Community Meetings is to
reinforce the use of the GOGI Tools and support positive
community experiences. We accomplish our objective
through the study of the GOGI Tools shared in Peer
Mentor Circles according to the GOGI Calendar of Study."

Circle Check In
Members of each Peer Mentor Circle share experiences, events, observations, or questions related to the understanding, use, and practice of the GOGI Tools. Each member is given the opportunity to "check in".

Weekly Tool Reading
(Volunteer/s To Share)
Volunteers are invited to read from any of the GOGI books, highlighting THIS WEEK'S TOOL, the KEY WORDS, CALENDAR STUDY DATES FOR THIS TOOL, STATEMENT OF OWNERSHIP and any other Tool details they find personally helpful.

Weekly Tool Experience
(Group Member Discussion)
Members of the group are invited to share personal experiences related to this or last week's Tool. Challenges in applying the Tool are also discussed. Open dialog includes all group members in equal sharing of talk time.

Quick Review
Members briefly review the Tool name, key words, statement of ownership and calendar dates on which this Tool is studied worldwide. Group members can contribute a few thoughts as to this Tool, and what they learned or experienced during this week's meeting.

Activity
(Time Permitting)
Understanding that activities often reinforce group members' engagement and understanding of the GOGI Tools, now is a great time to engage in an activity which can be created by the group, gleaned from GOGI materials, or utilized in prior PowerUp! groups.

Weekly Statement of Intention
Members of the group are encouraged to share one goal on which they will focus during the week. This could be as

simple as the intention that they will use this week's Tool more than once during a specific circumstance. It may be a commitment to read portions of a GOGI book, or to share their learning with someone else. It could be as simple as doing a good deed that goes unnoticed. Each member is encouraged to set one intention for the week.

The GOGI Pledge of Service
(Read Aloud)
"All students of GOGI unite with our GOGI Pledge of Service. This pledge defines our purpose and is repeated at the end of every PowerUp! Community Meeting. Remaining in your Peer Mentor Circles, each group will rotate leading the pledge for the larger group. As we close this PowerUp! Community Meeting, we unite as a community with our pledge to be of service. Please repeat after me:"

May our commitment (repeat)
To the study of GOGI (repeat)
Grant us the joy (repeat)
Of giving and receiving (repeat)
So our inner freedom (repeat)
May be of maximum service (repeat)
To those we love (repeat)
And infinite others (repeat)

Tidy Up Time
(Read Aloud)
"We thank you for participating in this weeks PowerUp!. Our next meeting will be held (day/time/place) and the tool to be discussed according to the GOGI Calendar will be the tool (refer to calendar). Please let us leave this room clean and tidy for the next group."

PowerUp! Community Meeting

PowerUp!
BELLY BREATHING

Hold This Meeting:
Second Week of Jan., April, July, Oct.

Remember: PowerUp! Meetings may be held any day of the week as long as they are held according to the GOGI Calendar of Study which begins on Monday. If there is a fifth Monday in the month, tools studied that month are to be reviewed. All tools are repeated four times each year. Therefore, there is no such thing as a "make up" or "catching up" or doing two tools in one week when a previous meeting is missed. The community of GOGI remains on calendar for all meetings, thereby uniting all studies everywhere.

Administrative Duties and Details
If there are announcements, administrative details, voting, or distribution of materials, these tasks are to be conducted before your meeting begins. (All peer mentor groups should be formed after admin duties and details.)

Peer Mentor Circles
(Read Aloud)
"PowerUp! and all GOGI studies are defined by our GOGI Calendar of Study and our Peer Mentor Circles. If we have not already done so, at this time we break from the larger group meeting into our Peer Mentor Circles of 5-12 participants."

Start Your Meeting
(Volunteer To Read Aloud In Peer Mentor Circles)
"The GOGI Tools are studied worldwide according to the GOGI Calendar of Study. We unite with others according to this schedule, so no one will feel they are alone in their effort to make positive decisions. We believe in everyone's ability to benefit from this positive community of individuals united on the GOGI Calendar of Study. Therefore, we call this PowerUp! BELLY BREATHING Meeting to order, and we join in the Tool being studied by students of GOGI everywhere."

Review of the Tools
(A Volunteer Recites Or Reads The GOGI Tools.)

BOSS OF MY BRAIN
BELLY BREATHING
FIVE SECOND LIGHTSWITCH
POSITIVE THOUGHTS
POSITIVE WORDS
POSITIVE ACTIONS
CLAIM RESPONSIBILITY
LET GO
FOR-GIVE
WHAT IF
REALITY CHECK
ULTIMATE FREEDOM

The PowerUp! Purpose
(Volunteer To Read)
"The objective of PowerUp! Community Meetings is to reinforce the use of the GOGI Tools and support positive community experiences. We accomplish our objective through the study of the GOGI Tools shared in Peer Mentor Circles according to the GOGI Calendar of Study."

Circle Check In

Members of each Peer Mentor Circle share experiences, events, observations, or questions related to the understanding, use, and practice of the GOGI Tools. Each member is given the opportunity to "check in".

Weekly Tool Reading
(Volunteer/s To Share)

Volunteers are invited to read from any of the GOGI books, highlighting THIS WEEK'S TOOL, the KEY WORDS, CALENDAR STUDY DATES FOR THIS TOOL, STATEMENT OF OWNERSHIP and any other Tool details they find personally helpful.

Weekly Tool Experience
(Group Member Discussion)

Members of the group are invited to share personal experiences related to this or last week's Tool. Challenges in applying the Tool are also discussed. Open dialog includes all group members in equal sharing of talk time.

Quick Review

Members briefly review the Tool name, key words, statement of ownership and calendar dates on which this Tool is studied worldwide. Group members can contribute a few thoughts as to this Tool, and what they learned or experienced during this week's meeting.

Activity
(Time Permitting)

Understanding that activities often reinforce group members' engagement and understanding of the GOGI Tools, now is a great time to engage in an activity which can be created by the group, gleaned from GOGI materials, or utilized in prior PowerUp! groups.

Weekly Statement of Intention

Members of the group are encouraged to share one goal on which they will focus during the week. This could be as

simple as the intention that they will use this week's Tool more than once during a specific circumstance. It may be a commitment to read portions of a GOGI book, or to share their learning with someone else. It could be as simple as doing a good deed that goes unnoticed. Each member is encouraged to set one intention for the week.

The GOGI Pledge of Service
(Read Aloud)

"All students of GOGI unite with our GOGI Pledge of Service. This pledge defines our purpose and is repeated at the end of every PowerUp! Community Meeting. Remaining in your Peer Mentor Circles, each group will rotate leading the pledge for the larger group. As we close this PowerUp! Community Meeting, we unite as a community with our pledge to be of service. Please repeat after me:"

May our commitment (repeat)
To the study of GOGI (repeat)
Grant us the joy (repeat)
Of giving and receiving (repeat)
So our inner freedom (repeat)
May be of maximum service (repeat)
To those we love (repeat)
And infinite others (repeat)

Tidy Up Time
(Read Aloud)

"We thank you for participating in this weeks PowerUp!. Our next meeting will be held (day/time/place) and the tool to be discussed according to the GOGI Calendar will be the tool (refer to calendar). Please let us leave this room clean and tidy for the next group."

PowerUp! Community Meeting

PowerUp!
FIVE SECOND LIGHTSWITCH

Hold This Meeting:
Third Week of Jan., April, July, Oct.

Remember: PowerUp! Meetings may be held any day of the week as long as they are held according to the GOGI Calendar of Study which begins on Monday. If there is a fifth Monday in the month, tools studied that month are to be reviewed. All tools are repeated four times each year. Therefore, there is no such thing as a "make up" or "catching up" or doing two tools in one week when a previous meeting is missed. The community of GOGI remains on calendar for all meetings, thereby uniting all studies everywhere.

Administrative Duties and Details
If there are announcements, administrative details, voting, or distribution of materials, these tasks are to be conducted before your meeting begins. (All peer mentor groups should be formed after admin duties and details.)

Peer Mentor Circles
(Read Aloud)
"PowerUp! and all GOGI studies are defined by our GOGI Calendar of Study and our Peer Mentor Circles. If we have not already done so, at this time we break from the larger group meeting into our Peer Mentor Circles of 5-12 participants."

Start Your Meeting
(Volunteer To Read Aloud In Peer Mentor Circles)
"The GOGI Tools are studied worldwide according to the GOGI Calendar of Study. We unite with others according to this schedule, so no one will feel they are alone in their effort to make positive decisions. We believe in everyone's ability to benefit from this positive community of individuals united on the GOGI Calendar of Study. Therefore, we call this PowerUp! FIVE SECOND LIGHTSWITCH Meeting to order, and we join in the Tool being studied by students of GOGI everywhere."

Review of the Tools
(A Volunteer Recites Or Reads The GOGI Tools.)

BOSS OF MY BRAIN
BELLY BREATHING
FIVE SECOND LIGHTSWITCH
POSITIVE THOUGHTS
POSITIVE WORDS
POSITIVE ACTIONS
CLAIM RESPONSIBILITY
LET GO
FOR-GIVE
WHAT IF
REALITY CHECK
ULTIMATE FREEDOM

The PowerUp! Purpose
(Volunteer To Read)
"The objective of PowerUp! Community Meetings is to reinforce the use of the GOGI Tools and support positive community experiences. We accomplish our objective through the study of the GOGI Tools shared in Peer Mentor Circles according to the GOGI Calendar of Study."

Circle Check In
Members of each Peer Mentor Circle share experiences, events, observations, or questions related to the understanding, use, and practice of the GOGI Tools. Each member is given the opportunity to "check in".

Weekly Tool Reading
(Volunteer/s To Share)
Volunteers are invited to read from any of the GOGI books, highlighting THIS WEEK'S TOOL, the KEY WORDS, CALENDAR STUDY DATES FOR THIS TOOL, STATEMENT OF OWNERSHIP and any other Tool details they find personally helpful.

Weekly Tool Experience
(Group Member Discussion)
Members of the group are invited to share personal experiences related to this or last week's Tool. Challenges in applying the Tool are also discussed. Open dialog includes all group members in equal sharing of talk time.

Quick Review
Members briefly review the Tool name, key words, statement of ownership and calendar dates on which this Tool is studied worldwide. Group members can contribute a few thoughts as to this Tool, and what they learned or experienced during this week's meeting.

Activity
(Time Permitting)
Understanding that activities often reinforce group members' engagement and understanding of the GOGI Tools, now is a great time to engage in an activity which can be created by the group, gleaned from GOGI materials, or utilized in prior PowerUp! groups.

Weekly Statement of Intention
Members of the group are encouraged to share one goal on which they will focus during the week. This could be as

simple as the intention that they will use this week's Tool more than once during a specific circumstance. It may be a commitment to read portions of a GOGI book, or to share their learning with someone else. It could be as simple as doing a good deed that goes unnoticed. Each member is encouraged to set one intention for the week.

The GOGI Pledge of Service
(Read Aloud)
"All students of GOGI unite with our GOGI Pledge of Service. This pledge defines our purpose and is repeated at the end of every PowerUp! Community Meeting. Remaining in your Peer Mentor Circles, each group will rotate leading the pledge for the larger group. As we close this PowerUp! Community Meeting, we unite as a community with our pledge to be of service. Please repeat after me:"

May our commitment (repeat)
To the study of GOGI (repeat)
Grant us the joy (repeat)
Of giving and receiving (repeat)
So our inner freedom (repeat)
May be of maximum service (repeat)
To those we love (repeat)
And infinite others (repeat)

Tidy Up Time
(Read Aloud)
"We thank you for participating in this weeks PowerUp!. Our next meeting will be held (day/time/place) and the tool to be discussed according to the GOGI Calendar will be the tool (refer to calendar). Please let us leave this room clean and tidy for the next group."

PowerUp! Community Meeting
PowerUp!
POSITIVE THOUGHTS
Hold This Meeting:
Fourth Week of Jan., April, July, Oct.

Remember: PowerUp! Meetings may be held any day of the week as long as they are held according to the GOGI Calendar of Study which begins on Monday. If there is a fifth Monday in the month, tools studied that month are to be reviewed. All tools are repeated four times each year. Therefore, there is no such thing as a "make up" or "catching up" or doing two tools in one week when a previous meeting is missed. The community of GOGI remains on calendar for all meetings, thereby uniting all studies everywhere.

Administrative Duties and Details
If there are announcements, administrative details, voting, or distribution of materials, these tasks are to be conducted before your meeting begins. (All peer mentor groups should be formed after admin duties and details.)

Peer Mentor Circles
(Read Aloud)
"PowerUp! and all GOGI studies are defined by our GOGI Calendar of Study and our Peer Mentor Circles. If we have not already done so, at this time we break from the larger group meeting into our Peer Mentor Circles of 5-12 participants."

Start Your Meeting
(Volunteer To Read Aloud In Peer Mentor Circles)
"The GOGI Tools are studied worldwide according to the GOGI Calendar of Study. We unite with others according to this schedule, so no one will feel they are alone in their effort to make positive decisions. We believe in everyone's ability to benefit from this positive community of individuals united on the GOGI Calendar of Study. Therefore, we call this PowerUp! POSITIVE THOUGHTS Meeting to order, and we join in the Tool being studied by students of GOGI everywhere."

Review of the Tools
(A Volunteer Recites Or Reads The GOGI Tools.)

BOSS OF MY BRAIN

BELLY BREATHING

FIVE SECOND LIGHTSWITCH

POSITIVE THOUGHTS

POSITIVE WORDS

POSITIVE ACTIONS

CLAIM RESPONSIBILITY

LET GO

FOR-GIVE

WHAT IF

REALITY CHECK

ULTIMATE FREEDOM

The PowerUp! Purpose
(Volunteer To Read)
"The objective of PowerUp! Community Meetings is to reinforce the use of the GOGI Tools and support positive community experiences. We accomplish our objective through the study of the GOGI Tools shared in Peer Mentor Circles according to the GOGI Calendar of Study."

Circle Check In
Members of each Peer Mentor Circle share experiences, events, observations, or questions related to the understanding, use, and practice of the GOGI Tools. Each member is given the opportunity to "check in".

Weekly Tool Reading
(Volunteer/s To Share)
Volunteers are invited to read from any of the GOGI books, highlighting THIS WEEK'S TOOL, the KEY WORDS, CALENDAR STUDY DATES FOR THIS TOOL, STATEMENT OF OWNERSHIP and any other Tool details they find personally helpful.

Weekly Tool Experience
(Group Member Discussion)
Members of the group are invited to share personal experiences related to this or last week's Tool. Challenges in applying the Tool are also discussed. Open dialog includes all group members in equal sharing of talk time.

Quick Review
Members briefly review the Tool name, key words, statement of ownership and calendar dates on which this Tool is studied worldwide. Group members can contribute a few thoughts as to this Tool, and what they learned or experienced during this week's meeting.

Activity
(Time Permitting)
Understanding that activities often reinforce group members' engagement and understanding of the GOGI Tools, now is a great time to engage in an activity which can be created by the group, gleaned from GOGI materials, or utilized in prior PowerUp! groups.

Weekly Statement of Intention
Members of the group are encouraged to share one goal on which they will focus during the week. This could be as

simple as the intention that they will use this week's Tool more than once during a specific circumstance. It may be a commitment to read portions of a GOGI book, or to share their learning with someone else. It could be as simple as doing a good deed that goes unnoticed. Each member is encouraged to set one intention for the week.

The GOGI Pledge of Service
(Read Aloud)

"All students of GOGI unite with our GOGI Pledge of Service. This pledge defines our purpose and is repeated at the end of every PowerUp! Community Meeting. Remaining in your Peer Mentor Circles, each group will rotate leading the pledge for the larger group. As we close this PowerUp! Community Meeting, we unite as a community with our pledge to be of service. Please repeat after me:"

May our commitment (repeat)
To the study of GOGI (repeat)
Grant us the joy (repeat)
Of giving and receiving (repeat)
So our inner freedom (repeat)
May be of maximum service (repeat)
To those we love (repeat)
And infinite others (repeat)

Tidy Up Time
(Read Aloud)

"We thank you for participating in this weeks PowerUp!. Our next meeting will be held (day/time/place) and the tool to be discussed according to the GOGI Calendar will be the tool (refer to calendar). Please let us leave this room clean and tidy for the next group."

PowerUp! Community Meeting

PowerUp!

POSITIVE WORDS

Hold This Meeting:
First Week of Feb.,May, Aug.,Nov.

Remember: PowerUp! Meetings may be held any day of the week as long as they are held according to the GOGI Calendar of Study which begins on Monday. If there is a fifth Monday in the month, tools studied that month are to be reviewed. All tools are repeated four times each year. Therefore, there is no such thing as a "make up" or "catching up" or doing two tools in one week when a previous meeting is missed. The community of GOGI remains on calendar for all meetings, thereby uniting all studies everywhere.

Administrative Duties and Details

If there are announcements, administrative details, voting, or distribution of materials, these tasks are to be conducted before your meeting begins. (All peer mentor groups should be formed after admin duties and details.)

Peer Mentor Circles

(Read Aloud)

"PowerUp! and all GOGI studies are defined by our GOGI Calendar of Study and our Peer Mentor Circles. If we have not already done so, at this time we break from the larger group meeting into our Peer Mentor Circles of 5-12 participants."

Start Your Meeting
(Volunteer To Read Aloud In Peer Mentor Circles)
"The GOGI Tools are studied worldwide according to the GOGI Calendar of Study. We unite with others according to this schedule, so no one will feel they are alone in their effort to make positive decisions. We believe in everyone's ability to benefit from this positive community of individuals united on the GOGI Calendar of Study. Therefore, we call this PowerUp! POSITIVE WORDS Meeting to order, and we join in the Tool being studied by students of GOGI everywhere."

Review of the Tools
(A Volunteer Recites Or Reads The GOGI Tools.)

BOSS OF MY BRAIN
BELLY BREATHING
FIVE SECOND LIGHTSWITCH
POSITIVE THOUGHTS
POSITIVE WORDS
POSITIVE ACTIONS
CLAIM RESPONSIBILITY
LET GO
FOR-GIVE
WHAT IF
REALITY CHECK
ULTIMATE FREEDOM

The PowerUp! Purpose
(Volunteer To Read)
"The objective of PowerUp! Community Meetings is to reinforce the use of the GOGI Tools and support positive community experiences. We accomplish our objective through the study of the GOGI Tools shared in Peer Mentor Circles according to the GOGI Calendar of Study."

Circle Check In

Members of each Peer Mentor Circle share experiences, events, observations, or questions related to the understanding, use, and practice of the GOGI Tools. Each member is given the opportunity to "check in".

Weekly Tool Reading
(Volunteer/s To Share)

Volunteers are invited to read from any of the GOGI books, highlighting THIS WEEK'S TOOL, the KEY WORDS, CALENDAR STUDY DATES FOR THIS TOOL, STATEMENT OF OWNERSHIP and any other Tool details they find personally helpful.

Weekly Tool Experience
(Group Member Discussion)

Members of the group are invited to share personal experiences related to this or last week's Tool. Challenges in applying the Tool are also discussed. Open dialog includes all group members in equal sharing of talk time.

Quick Review

Members briefly review the Tool name, key words, statement of ownership and calendar dates on which this Tool is studied worldwide. Group members can contribute a few thoughts as to this Tool, and what they learned or experienced during this week's meeting.

Activity
(Time Permitting)

Understanding that activities often reinforce group members' engagement and understanding of the GOGI Tools, now is a great time to engage in an activity which can be created by the group, gleaned from GOGI materials, or utilized in prior PowerUp! groups.

Weekly Statement of Intention

Members of the group are encouraged to share one goal on which they will focus during the week. This could be as

simple as the intention that they will use this week's Tool more than once during a specific circumstance. It may be a commitment to read portions of a GOGI book, or to share their learning with someone else. It could be as simple as doing a good deed that goes unnoticed. Each member is encouraged to set one intention for the week.

The GOGI Pledge of Service
(Read Aloud)

"All students of GOGI unite with our GOGI Pledge of Service. This pledge defines our purpose and is repeated at the end of every PowerUp! Community Meeting. Remaining in your Peer Mentor Circles, each group will rotate leading the pledge for the larger group. As we close this PowerUp! Community Meeting, we unite as a community with our pledge to be of service. Please repeat after me:"

May our commitment (repeat)
To the study of GOGI (repeat)
Grant us the joy (repeat)
Of giving and receiving (repeat)
So our inner freedom (repeat)
May be of maximum service (repeat)
To those we love (repeat)
And infinite others (repeat)

Tidy Up Time
(Read Aloud)

"We thank you for participating in this weeks PowerUp!. Our next meeting will be held (day/time/place) and the tool to be discussed according to the GOGI Calendar will be the tool (refer to calendar). Please let us leave this room clean and tidy for the next group."

PowerUp! Community Meeting

PowerUp!
POSITIVE ACTIONS

Hold This Meeting:
Second Week of Feb.,May, Aug.,Nov.

Remember: PowerUp! Meetings may be held any day of the week as long as they are held according to the GOGI Calendar of Study which begins on Monday. If there is a fifth Monday in the month, tools studied that month are to be reviewed. All tools are repeated four times each year. Therefore, there is no such thing as a "make up" or "catching up" or doing two tools in one week when a previous meeting is missed. The community of GOGI remains on calendar for all meetings, thereby uniting all studies everywhere.

Administrative Duties and Details

If there are announcements, administrative details, voting, or distribution of materials, these tasks are to be conducted before your meeting begins. (All peer mentor groups should be formed after admin duties and details.)

Peer Mentor Circles

(Read Aloud)

"PowerUp! and all GOGI studies are defined by our GOGI Calendar of Study and our Peer Mentor Circles. If we have not already done so, at this time we break from the larger group meeting into our Peer Mentor Circles of 5-12 participants."

Start Your Meeting

(Volunteer To Read Aloud In Peer Mentor Circles)

"The GOGI Tools are studied worldwide according to the GOGI Calendar of Study. We unite with others according to this schedule, so no one will feel they are alone in their effort to make positive decisions. We believe in everyone's ability to benefit from this positive community of individuals united on the GOGI Calendar of Study. Therefore, we call this PowerUp! POSITIVE ACTIONS Meeting to order, and we join in the Tool being studied by students of GOGI everywhere."

Review of the Tools

(A Volunteer Recites Or Reads The GOGI Tools.)

BOSS OF MY BRAIN
BELLY BREATHING
FIVE SECOND LIGHTSWITCH
POSITIVE THOUGHTS
POSITIVE WORDS
POSITIVE ACTIONS
CLAIM RESPONSIBILITY
LET GO
FOR-GIVE
WHAT IF
REALITY CHECK
ULTIMATE FREEDOM

The PowerUp! Purpose

(Volunteer To Read)

"The objective of PowerUp! Community Meetings is to reinforce the use of the GOGI Tools and support positive community experiences. We accomplish our objective through the study of the GOGI Tools shared in Peer Mentor Circles according to the GOGI Calendar of Study."

Circle Check In

Members of each Peer Mentor Circle share experiences, events, observations, or questions related to the understanding, use, and practice of the GOGI Tools. Each member is given the opportunity to "check in".

Weekly Tool Reading
(Volunteer/s To Share)

Volunteers are invited to read from any of the GOGI books, highlighting THIS WEEK'S TOOL, the KEY WORDS, CALENDAR STUDY DATES FOR THIS TOOL, STATEMENT OF OWNERSHIP and any other Tool details they find personally helpful.

Weekly Tool Experience
(Group Member Discussion)

Members of the group are invited to share personal experiences related to this or last week's Tool. Challenges in applying the Tool are also discussed. Open dialog includes all group members in equal sharing of talk time.

Quick Review

Members briefly review the Tool name, key words, statement of ownership and calendar dates on which this Tool is studied worldwide. Group members can contribute a few thoughts as to this Tool, and what they learned or experienced during this week's meeting.

Activity
(Time Permitting)

Understanding that activities often reinforce group members' engagement and understanding of the GOGI Tools, now is a great time to engage in an activity which can be created by the group, gleaned from GOGI materials, or utilized in prior PowerUp! groups.

Weekly Statement of Intention

Members of the group are encouraged to share one goal on which they will focus during the week. This could be as

simple as the intention that they will use this week's Tool more than once during a specific circumstance. It may be a commitment to read portions of a GOGI book, or to share their learning with someone else. It could be as simple as doing a good deed that goes unnoticed. Each member is encouraged to set one intention for the week.

The GOGI Pledge of Service
(Read Aloud)

"All students of GOGI unite with our GOGI Pledge of Service. This pledge defines our purpose and is repeated at the end of every PowerUp! Community Meeting. Remaining in your Peer Mentor Circles, each group will rotate leading the pledge for the larger group. As we close this PowerUp! Community Meeting, we unite as a community with our pledge to be of service. Please repeat after me:"

May our commitment (repeat)
To the study of GOGI (repeat)
Grant us the joy (repeat)
Of giving and receiving (repeat)
So our inner freedom (repeat)
May be of maximum service (repeat)
To those we love (repeat)
And infinite others (repeat)

Tidy Up Time
(Read Aloud)

"We thank you for participating in this weeks PowerUp!. Our next meeting will be held (day/time/place) and the tool to be discussed according to the GOGI Calendar will be the tool (refer to calendar). Please let us leave this room clean and tidy for the next group."

PowerUp! Community Meeting

PowerUp!
CLAIM RESPONSIBILITY

Hold This Meeting:
Third Week of Feb.,May, Aug.,Nov.

Remember: PowerUp! Meetings may be held any day of the week as long as they are held according to the GOGI Calendar of Study which begins on Monday. If there is a fifth Monday in the month, tools studied that month are to be reviewed. All tools are repeated four times each year. Therefore, there is no such thing as a "make up" or "catching up" or doing two tools in one week when a previous meeting is missed. The community of GOGI remains on calendar for all meetings, thereby uniting all studies everywhere.

Administrative Duties and Details

If there are announcements, administrative details, voting, or distribution of materials, these tasks are to be conducted before your meeting begins. (All peer mentor groups should be formed after admin duties and details.)

Peer Mentor Circles

(Read Aloud)

"PowerUp! and all GOGI studies are defined by our GOGI Calendar of Study and our Peer Mentor Circles. If we have not already done so, at this time we break from the larger group meeting into our Peer Mentor Circles of 5-12 participants."

Start Your Meeting
(Volunteer To Read Aloud In Peer Mentor Circles)
"The GOGI Tools are studied worldwide according to the GOGI Calendar of Study. We unite with others according to this schedule, so no one will feel they are alone in their effort to make positive decisions. We believe in everyone's ability to benefit from this positive community of individuals united on the GOGI Calendar of Study. Therefore, we call this PowerUp! CLAIM RESPONSIBILITY Meeting to order, and we join in the Tool being studied by students of GOGI everywhere."

Review of the Tools
(A Volunteer Recites Or Reads The GOGI Tools.)

BOSS OF MY BRAIN
BELLY BREATHING
FIVE SECOND LIGHTSWITCH
POSITIVE THOUGHTS
POSITIVE WORDS
POSITIVE ACTIONS
CLAIM RESPONSIBILITY
LET GO
FOR-GIVE
WHAT IF
REALITY CHECK
ULTIMATE FREEDOM

The PowerUp! Purpose
(Volunteer To Read)
"The objective of PowerUp! Community Meetings is to reinforce the use of the GOGI Tools and support positive community experiences. We accomplish our objective through the study of the GOGI Tools shared in Peer Mentor Circles according to the GOGI Calendar of Study."

Circle Check In

Members of each Peer Mentor Circle share experiences, events, observations, or questions related to the understanding, use, and practice of the GOGI Tools. Each member is given the opportunity to "check in".

Weekly Tool Reading

(Volunteer/s To Share)

Volunteers are invited to read from any of the GOGI books, highlighting THIS WEEK'S TOOL, the KEY WORDS, CALENDAR STUDY DATES FOR THIS TOOL, STATEMENT OF OWNERSHIP and any other Tool details they find personally helpful.

Weekly Tool Experience

(Group Member Discussion)

Members of the group are invited to share personal experiences related to this or last week's Tool. Challenges in applying the Tool are also discussed. Open dialog includes all group members in equal sharing of talk time.

Quick Review

Members briefly review the Tool name, key words, statement of ownership and calendar dates on which this Tool is studied worldwide. Group members can contribute a few thoughts as to this Tool, and what they learned or experienced during this week's meeting.

Activity

(Time Permitting)

Understanding that activities often reinforce group members' engagement and understanding of the GOGI Tools, now is a great time to engage in an activity which can be created by the group, gleaned from GOGI materials, or utilized in prior PowerUp! groups.

Weekly Statement of Intention

Members of the group are encouraged to share one goal on which they will focus during the week. This could be as

simple as the intention that they will use this week's Tool more than once during a specific circumstance. It may be a commitment to read portions of a GOGI book, or to share their learning with someone else. It could be as simple as doing a good deed that goes unnoticed. Each member is encouraged to set one intention for the week.

The GOGI Pledge of Service
(Read Aloud)

"All students of GOGI unite with our GOGI Pledge of Service. This pledge defines our purpose and is repeated at the end of every PowerUp! Community Meeting. Remaining in your Peer Mentor Circles, each group will rotate leading the pledge for the larger group. As we close this PowerUp! Community Meeting, we unite as a community with our pledge to be of service. Please repeat after me:"

May our commitment (repeat)
To the study of GOGI (repeat)
Grant us the joy (repeat)
Of giving and receiving (repeat)
So our inner freedom (repeat)
May be of maximum service (repeat)
To those we love (repeat)
And infinite others (repeat)

Tidy Up Time
(Read Aloud)

"We thank you for participating in this weeks PowerUp!. Our next meeting will be held (day/time/place) and the tool to be discussed according to the GOGI Calendar will be the tool (refer to calendar). Please let us leave this room clean and tidy for the next group."

PowerUp! Community Meeting

PowerUp!

LET GO

Hold This Meeting:
Fourth Week of Feb.,May, Aug.,Nov.

Remember: PowerUp! Meetings may be held any day of the week as long as they are held according to the GOGI Calendar of Study which begins on Monday. If there is a fifth Monday in the month, tools studied that month are to be reviewed. All tools are repeated four times each year. Therefore, there is no such thing as a "make up" or "catching up" or doing two tools in one week when a previous meeting is missed. The community of GOGI remains on calendar for all meetings, thereby uniting all studies everywhere.

Administrative Duties and Details

If there are announcements, administrative details, voting, or distribution of materials, these tasks are to be conducted before your meeting begins. (All peer mentor groups should be formed after admin duties and details.)

Peer Mentor Circles

(Read Aloud)

"PowerUp! and all GOGI studies are defined by our GOGI Calendar of Study and our Peer Mentor Circles. If we have not already done so, at this time we break from the larger group meeting into our Peer Mentor Circles of 5-12 participants."

Start Your Meeting
(Volunteer To Read Aloud In Peer Mentor Circles)
"The GOGI Tools are studied worldwide according to the GOGI Calendar of Study. We unite with others according to this schedule, so no one will feel they are alone in their effort to make positive decisions. We believe in everyone's ability to benefit from this positive community of individuals united on the GOGI Calendar of Study. Therefore, we call this PowerUp! LET GO Meeting to order, and we join in the Tool being studied by students of GOGI everywhere."

Review of the Tools
(A Volunteer Recites Or Reads The GOGI Tools.)

BOSS OF MY BRAIN
BELLY BREATHING
FIVE SECOND LIGHTSWITCH
POSITIVE THOUGHTS
POSITIVE WORDS
POSITIVE ACTIONS
CLAIM RESPONSIBILITY
LET GO
FOR-GIVE
WHAT IF
REALITY CHECK
ULTIMATE FREEDOM

The PowerUp! Purpose
(Volunteer To Read)
"The objective of PowerUp! Community Meetings is to reinforce the use of the GOGI Tools and support positive community experiences. We accomplish our objective through the study of the GOGI Tools shared in Peer Mentor Circles according to the GOGI Calendar of Study."

Circle Check In
Members of each Peer Mentor Circle share experiences, events, observations, or questions related to the understanding, use, and practice of the GOGI Tools. Each member is given the opportunity to "check in".

Weekly Tool Reading
(Volunteer/s To Share)
Volunteers are invited to read from any of the GOGI books, highlighting THIS WEEK'S TOOL, the KEY WORDS, CALENDAR STUDY DATES FOR THIS TOOL, STATEMENT OF OWNERSHIP and any other Tool details they find personally helpful.

Weekly Tool Experience
(Group Member Discussion)
Members of the group are invited to share personal experiences related to this or last week's Tool. Challenges in applying the Tool are also discussed. Open dialog includes all group members in equal sharing of talk time.

Quick Review
Members briefly review the Tool name, key words, statement of ownership and calendar dates on which this Tool is studied worldwide. Group members can contribute a few thoughts as to this Tool, and what they learned or experienced during this week's meeting.

Activity
(Time Permitting)
Understanding that activities often reinforce group members' engagement and understanding of the GOGI Tools, now is a great time to engage in an activity which can be created by the group, gleaned from GOGI materials, or utilized in prior PowerUp! groups.

Weekly Statement of Intention
Members of the group are encouraged to share one goal on which they will focus during the week. This could be as

simple as the intention that they will use this week's Tool more than once during a specific circumstance. It may be a commitment to read portions of a GOGI book, or to share their learning with someone else. It could be as simple as doing a good deed that goes unnoticed. Each member is encouraged to set one intention for the week.

The GOGI Pledge of Service
(Read Aloud)
"All students of GOGI unite with our GOGI Pledge of Service. This pledge defines our purpose and is repeated at the end of every PowerUp! Community Meeting. Remaining in your Peer Mentor Circles, each group will rotate leading the pledge for the larger group. As we close this PowerUp! Community Meeting, we unite as a community with our pledge to be of service. Please repeat after me:"

May our commitment (repeat)
To the study of GOGI (repeat)
Grant us the joy (repeat)
Of giving and receiving (repeat)
So our inner freedom (repeat)
May be of maximum service (repeat)
To those we love (repeat)
And infinite others (repeat)

Tidy Up Time
(Read Aloud)
"We thank you for participating in this weeks PowerUp!. Our next meeting will be held (day/time/place) and the tool to be discussed according to the GOGI Calendar will be the tool (refer to calendar). Please let us leave this room clean and tidy for the next group."

PowerUp! Community Meeting

PowerUp!

FOR-GIVE

Hold This Meeting:
First Week of March, June, Sept.,Dec.

Remember: PowerUp! Meetings may be held any day of the week as long as they are held according to the GOGI Calendar of Study which begins on Monday. If there is a fifth Monday in the month, tools studied that month are to be reviewed. All tools are repeated four times each year. Therefore, there is no such thing as a "make up" or "catching up" or doing two tools in one week when a previous meeting is missed. The community of GOGI remains on calendar for all meetings, thereby uniting all studies everywhere.

Administrative Duties and Details

If there are announcements, administrative details, voting, or distribution of materials, these tasks are to be conducted before your meeting begins. (All peer mentor groups should be formed after admin duties and details.)

Peer Mentor Circles

(Read Aloud)

"PowerUp! and all GOGI studies are defined by our GOGI Calendar of Study and our Peer Mentor Circles. If we have not already done so, at this time we break from the larger group meeting into our Peer Mentor Circles of 5-12 participants."

Start Your Meeting
(Volunteer To Read Aloud In Peer Mentor Circles)
"The GOGI Tools are studied worldwide according to the GOGI Calendar of Study. We unite with others according to this schedule, so no one will feel they are alone in their effort to make positive decisions. We believe in everyone's ability to benefit from this positive community of individuals united on the GOGI Calendar of Study. Therefore, we call this PowerUp! FOR-GIVE Meeting to order, and we join in the Tool being studied by students of GOGI everywhere."

Review of the Tools
(A Volunteer Recites Or Reads The GOGI Tools.)

BOSS OF MY BRAIN
BELLY BREATHING
FIVE SECOND LIGHTSWITCH
POSITIVE THOUGHTS
POSITIVE WORDS
POSITIVE ACTIONS
CLAIM RESPONSIBILITY
LET GO
FOR-GIVE
WHAT IF
REALITY CHECK
ULTIMATE FREEDOM

The PowerUp! Purpose
(Volunteer To Read)
"The objective of PowerUp! Community Meetings is to reinforce the use of the GOGI Tools and support positive community experiences. We accomplish our objective through the study of the GOGI Tools shared in Peer Mentor Circles according to the GOGI Calendar of Study."

Circle Check In

Members of each Peer Mentor Circle share experiences, events, observations, or questions related to the understanding, use, and practice of the GOGI Tools. Each member is given the opportunity to "check in".

Weekly Tool Reading
(Volunteer/s To Share)

Volunteers are invited to read from any of the GOGI books, highlighting THIS WEEK'S TOOL, the KEY WORDS, CALENDAR STUDY DATES FOR THIS TOOL, STATEMENT OF OWNERSHIP and any other Tool details they find personally helpful.

Weekly Tool Experience
(Group Member Discussion)

Members of the group are invited to share personal experiences related to this or last week's Tool. Challenges in applying the Tool are also discussed. Open dialog includes all group members in equal sharing of talk time.

Quick Review

Members briefly review the Tool name, key words, statement of ownership and calendar dates on which this Tool is studied worldwide. Group members can contribute a few thoughts as to this Tool, and what they learned or experienced during this week's meeting.

Activity
(Time Permitting)

Understanding that activities often reinforce group members' engagement and understanding of the GOGI Tools, now is a great time to engage in an activity which can be created by the group, gleaned from GOGI materials, or utilized in prior PowerUp! groups.

Weekly Statement of Intention

Members of the group are encouraged to share one goal on which they will focus during the week. This could be as

simple as the intention that they will use this week's Tool more than once during a specific circumstance. It may be a commitment to read portions of a GOGI book, or to share their learning with someone else. It could be as simple as doing a good deed that goes unnoticed. Each member is encouraged to set one intention for the week.

The GOGI Pledge of Service
(Read Aloud)

"All students of GOGI unite with our GOGI Pledge of Service. This pledge defines our purpose and is repeated at the end of every PowerUp! Community Meeting. Remaining in your Peer Mentor Circles, each group will rotate leading the pledge for the larger group. As we close this PowerUp! Community Meeting, we unite as a community with our pledge to be of service. Please repeat after me:"

May our commitment (repeat)
To the study of GOGI (repeat)
Grant us the joy (repeat)
Of giving and receiving (repeat)
So our inner freedom (repeat)
May be of maximum service (repeat)
To those we love (repeat)
And infinite others (repeat)

Tidy Up Time
(Read Aloud)

"We thank you for participating in this weeks PowerUp!. Our next meeting will be held (day/time/place) and the tool to be discussed according to the GOGI Calendar will be the tool (refer to calendar). Please let us leave this room clean and tidy for the next group."

PowerUp! Community Meeting

PowerUp!

WHAT IF

Hold This Meeting:
Second Week of March, June, Sept, Dec.

Remember: PowerUp! Meetings may be held any day of the week as long as they are held according to the GOGI Calendar of Study which begins on Monday. If there is a fifth Monday in the month, tools studied that month are to be reviewed. All tools are repeated four times each year. Therefore, there is no such thing as a "make up" or "catching up" or doing two tools in one week when a previous meeting is missed. The community of GOGI remains on calendar for all meetings, thereby uniting all studies everywhere.

Administrative Duties and Details

If there are announcements, administrative details, voting, or distribution of materials, these tasks are to be conducted before your meeting begins. (All peer mentor groups should be formed after admin duties and details.)

Peer Mentor Circles

(Read Aloud)

"PowerUp! and all GOGI studies are defined by our GOGI Calendar of Study and our Peer Mentor Circles. If we have not already done so, at this time we break from the larger group meeting into our Peer Mentor Circles of 5-12 participants."

Start Your Meeting
(Volunteer To Read Aloud In Peer Mentor Circles)
"The GOGI Tools are studied worldwide according to the GOGI Calendar of Study. We unite with others according to this schedule, so no one will feel they are alone in their effort to make positive decisions. We believe in everyone's ability to benefit from this positive community of individuals united on the GOGI Calendar of Study. Therefore, we call this PowerUp! WHAT IF Meeting to order, and we join in the Tool being studied by students of GOGI everywhere."

Review of the Tools
(A Volunteer Recites Or Reads The GOGI Tools.)
BOSS OF MY BRAIN
BELLY BREATHING
FIVE SECOND LIGHTSWITCH
POSITIVE THOUGHTS
POSITIVE WORDS
POSITIVE ACTIONS
CLAIM RESPONSIBILITY
LET GO
FOR-GIVE
WHAT IF
REALITY CHECK
ULTIMATE FREEDOM

The PowerUp! Purpose
(Volunteer To Read)
"The objective of PowerUp! Community Meetings is to reinforce the use of the GOGI Tools and support positive community experiences. We accomplish our objective through the study of the GOGI Tools shared in Peer Mentor Circles according to the GOGI Calendar of Study."

Circle Check In
Members of each Peer Mentor Circle share experiences, events, observations, or questions related to the understanding, use, and practice of the GOGI Tools. Each member is given the opportunity to "check in".

Weekly Tool Reading
(Volunteer/s To Share)
Volunteers are invited to read from any of the GOGI books, highlighting THIS WEEK'S TOOL, the KEY WORDS, CALENDAR STUDY DATES FOR THIS TOOL, STATEMENT OF OWNERSHIP and any other Tool details they find personally helpful.

Weekly Tool Experience
(Group Member Discussion)
Members of the group are invited to share personal experiences related to this or last week's Tool. Challenges in applying the Tool are also discussed. Open dialog includes all group members in equal sharing of talk time.

Quick Review
Members briefly review the Tool name, key words, statement of ownership and calendar dates on which this Tool is studied worldwide. Group members can contribute a few thoughts as to this Tool, and what they learned or experienced during this week's meeting.

Activity
(Time Permitting)
Understanding that activities often reinforce group members' engagement and understanding of the GOGI Tools, now is a great time to engage in an activity which can be created by the group, gleaned from GOGI materials, or utilized in prior PowerUp! groups.

Weekly Statement of Intention
Members of the group are encouraged to share one goal on which they will focus during the week. This could be as

simple as the intention that they will use this week's Tool more than once during a specific circumstance. It may be a commitment to read portions of a GOGI book, or to share their learning with someone else. It could be as simple as doing a good deed that goes unnoticed. Each member is encouraged to set one intention for the week.

The GOGI Pledge of Service
(Read Aloud)
"All students of GOGI unite with our GOGI Pledge of Service. This pledge defines our purpose and is repeated at the end of every PowerUp! Community Meeting. Remaining in your Peer Mentor Circles, each group will rotate leading the pledge for the larger group. As we close this PowerUp! Community Meeting, we unite as a community with our pledge to be of service. Please repeat after me:"

May our commitment (repeat)
To the study of GOGI (repeat)
Grant us the joy (repeat)
Of giving and receiving (repeat)
So our inner freedom (repeat)
May be of maximum service (repeat)
To those we love (repeat)
And infinite others (repeat)

Tidy Up Time
(Read Aloud)
"We thank you for participating in this weeks PowerUp!. Our next meeting will be held (day/time/place) and the tool to be discussed according to the GOGI Calendar will be the tool (refer to calendar). Please let us leave this room clean and tidy for the next group."

PowerUp! Community Meeting

PowerUp!
REALITY CHECK

Hold This Meeting:
Third Week of March, June, Sept., Dec.

Remember: PowerUp! Meetings may be held any day of the week as long as they are held according to the GOGI Calendar of Study which begins on Monday. If there is a fifth Monday in the month, tools studied that month are to be reviewed. All tools are repeated four times each year. Therefore, there is no such thing as a "make up" or "catching up" or doing two tools in one week when a previous meeting is missed. The community of GOGI remains on calendar for all meetings, thereby uniting all studies everywhere.

Administrative Duties and Details

If there are announcements, administrative details, voting, or distribution of materials, these tasks are to be conducted before your meeting begins. (All peer mentor groups should be formed after admin duties and details.)

Peer Mentor Circles

(Read Aloud)

"PowerUp! and all GOGI studies are defined by our GOGI Calendar of Study and our Peer Mentor Circles. If we have not already done so, at this time we break from the larger group meeting into our Peer Mentor Circles of 5-12 participants."

Start Your Meeting
(Volunteer To Read Aloud In Peer Mentor Circles)
"The GOGI Tools are studied worldwide according to the GOGI Calendar of Study. We unite with others according to this schedule, so no one will feel they are alone in their effort to make positive decisions. We believe in everyone's ability to benefit from this positive community of individuals united on the GOGI Calendar of Study. Therefore, we call this PowerUp! REALITY CHECK Meeting to order, and we join in the Tool being studied by students of GOGI everywhere."

Review of the Tools
(A Volunteer Recites Or Reads The GOGI Tools.)

BOSS OF MY BRAIN
BELLY BREATHING
FIVE SECOND LIGHTSWITCH
POSITIVE THOUGHTS
POSITIVE WORDS
POSITIVE ACTIONS
CLAIM RESPONSIBILITY
LET GO
FOR-GIVE
WHAT IF
REALITY CHECK
ULTIMATE FREEDOM

The PowerUp! Purpose
(Volunteer To Read)
"The objective of PowerUp! Community Meetings is to reinforce the use of the GOGI Tools and support positive community experiences. We accomplish our objective through the study of the GOGI Tools shared in Peer Mentor Circles according to the GOGI Calendar of Study."

Circle Check In

Members of each Peer Mentor Circle share experiences, events, observations, or questions related to the understanding, use, and practice of the GOGI Tools. Each member is given the opportunity to "check in".

Weekly Tool Reading

(Volunteer/s To Share)

Volunteers are invited to read from any of the GOGI books, highlighting THIS WEEK'S TOOL, the KEY WORDS, CALENDAR STUDY DATES FOR THIS TOOL, STATEMENT OF OWNERSHIP and any other Tool details they find personally helpful.

Weekly Tool Experience

(Group Member Discussion)

Members of the group are invited to share personal experiences related to this or last week's Tool. Challenges in applying the Tool are also discussed. Open dialog includes all group members in equal sharing of talk time.

Quick Review

Members briefly review the Tool name, key words, statement of ownership and calendar dates on which this Tool is studied worldwide. Group members can contribute a few thoughts as to this Tool, and what they learned or experienced during this week's meeting.

Activity

(Time Permitting)

Understanding that activities often reinforce group members' engagement and understanding of the GOGI Tools, now is a great time to engage in an activity which can be created by the group, gleaned from GOGI materials, or utilized in prior PowerUp! groups.

Weekly Statement of Intention

Members of the group are encouraged to share one goal on which they will focus during the week. This could be as

simple as the intention that they will use this week's Tool more than once during a specific circumstance. It may be a commitment to read portions of a GOGI book, or to share their learning with someone else. It could be as simple as doing a good deed that goes unnoticed. Each member is encouraged to set one intention for the week.

The GOGI Pledge of Service
(Read Aloud)

"All students of GOGI unite with our GOGI Pledge of Service. This pledge defines our purpose and is repeated at the end of every PowerUp! Community Meeting. Remaining in your Peer Mentor Circles, each group will rotate leading the pledge for the larger group. As we close this PowerUp! Community Meeting, we unite as a community with our pledge to be of service. Please repeat after me:"

May our commitment (repeat)
To the study of GOGI (repeat)
Grant us the joy (repeat)
Of giving and receiving (repeat)
So our inner freedom (repeat)
May be of maximum service (repeat)
To those we love (repeat)
And infinite others (repeat)

Tidy Up Time
(Read Aloud)

"We thank you for participating in this weeks PowerUp!. Our next meeting will be held (day/time/place) and the tool to be discussed according to the GOGI Calendar will be the tool (refer to calendar). Please let us leave this room clean and tidy for the next group."

PowerUp! Community Meeting
PowerUp!
ULTIMATE FREEDOM
Hold This Meeting:
Fourth Week of March, June, Sept.,Dec.

Remember: PowerUp! Meetings may be held any day of the week as long as they are held according to the GOGI Calendar of Study which begins on Monday. If there is a fifth Monday in the month, tools studied that month are to be reviewed. All tools are repeated four times each year. Therefore, there is no such thing as a "make up" or "catching up" or doing two tools in one week when a previous meeting is missed. The community of GOGI remains on calendar for all meetings, thereby uniting all studies everywhere.

Administrative Duties and Details
If there are announcements, administrative details, voting, or distribution of materials, these tasks are to be conducted before your meeting begins. (All peer mentor groups should be formed after admin duties and details.)

Peer Mentor Circles
(Read Aloud)
"PowerUp! and all GOGI studies are defined by our GOGI Calendar of Study and our Peer Mentor Circles. If we have not already done so, at this time we break from the larger group meeting into our Peer Mentor Circles of 5-12 participants."

Start Your Meeting
(Volunteer To Read Aloud In Peer Mentor Circles)
"The GOGI Tools are studied worldwide according to the
GOGI Calendar of Study. We unite with others according
to this schedule, so no one will feel they are alone in
their effort to make positive decisions. We believe in
everyone's ability to benefit from this positive community
of individuals united on the GOGI Calendar of Study.
Therefore, we call this PowerUp! ULTIMATE FREEDOM
Meeting to order, and we join in the Tool being studied by
students of GOGI everywhere."

Review of the Tools
(A Volunteer Recites Or Reads The GOGI Tools.)

BOSS OF MY BRAIN
BELLY BREATHING
FIVE SECOND LIGHTSWITCH
POSITIVE THOUGHTS
POSITIVE WORDS
POSITIVE ACTIONS
CLAIM RESPONSIBILITY
LET GO
FOR-GIVE
WHAT IF
REALITY CHECK
ULTIMATE FREEDOM

The PowerUp! Purpose
(Volunteer To Read)
"The objective of PowerUp! Community Meetings is to
reinforce the use of the GOGI Tools and support positive
community experiences. We accomplish our objective
through the study of the GOGI Tools shared in Peer
Mentor Circles according to the GOGI Calendar of Study."

Circle Check In

Members of each Peer Mentor Circle share experiences, events, observations, or questions related to the understanding, use, and practice of the GOGI Tools. Each member is given the opportunity to "check in".

Weekly Tool Reading

(Volunteer/s To Share)

Volunteers are invited to read from any of the GOGI books, highlighting THIS WEEK'S TOOL, the KEY WORDS, CALENDAR STUDY DATES FOR THIS TOOL, STATEMENT OF OWNERSHIP and any other Tool details they find personally helpful.

Weekly Tool Experience

(Group Member Discussion)

Members of the group are invited to share personal experiences related to this or last week's Tool. Challenges in applying the Tool are also discussed. Open dialog includes all group members in equal sharing of talk time.

Quick Review

Members briefly review the Tool name, key words, statement of ownership and calendar dates on which this Tool is studied worldwide. Group members can contribute a few thoughts as to this Tool, and what they learned or experienced during this week's meeting.

Activity

(Time Permitting)

Understanding that activities often reinforce group members' engagement and understanding of the GOGI Tools, now is a great time to engage in an activity which can be created by the group, gleaned from GOGI materials, or utilized in prior PowerUp! groups.

Weekly Statement of Intention

Members of the group are encouraged to share one goal on which they will focus during the week. This could be as

simple as the intention that they will use this week's Tool more than once during a specific circumstance. It may be a commitment to read portions of a GOGI book, or to share their learning with someone else. It could be as simple as doing a good deed that goes unnoticed. Each member is encouraged to set one intention for the week.

The GOGI Pledge of Service
(Read Aloud)
"All students of GOGI unite with our GOGI Pledge of Service. This pledge defines our purpose and is repeated at the end of every PowerUp! Community Meeting. Remaining in your Peer Mentor Circles, each group will rotate leading the pledge for the larger group. As we close this PowerUp! Community Meeting, we unite as a community with our pledge to be of service. Please repeat after me:"

May our commitment (repeat)
To the study of GOGI (repeat)
Grant us the joy (repeat)
Of giving and receiving (repeat)
So our inner freedom (repeat)
May be of maximum service (repeat)
To those we love (repeat)
And infinite others (repeat)

Tidy Up Time
(Read Aloud)
"We thank you for participating in this weeks PowerUp!. Our next meeting will be held (day/time/place) and the tool to be discussed according to the GOGI Calendar will be the tool (refer to calendar). Please let us leave this room clean and tidy for the next group."

Getting Out by Going In (GOGI) www.GettingOutByGoingIn.org

PowerUp! Community Meeting

PowerUp!

Tool Review Meeting

Hold this Meeting: After Every 15 Meetings

Building a skill takes repetition and concentration. After every 15 meetings, it is important to review what your Peer Mentor Circle has experienced. In this review, you solidify the learning. This Tool Review Meeting can be one of your most empowering, fun and energetic meetings as each of the members of the group are encouraged to share their journey and their daily application of GOGI Tools.

During the review process, please be mindful that your internal freedom is enhanced by your willingness to reach beyond your own needs and share the best of you with those around you. You truly are a solution for your community and this Tool Review Meeting should help you realize how to make that a reality.

Acknowledging the progress made by group members can encourage continuation along that path. For this reason we take the time to celebrate successes. When we nurture the attitude and practice of reaching goals, we are encouraged and we encourage others to do the same.

Success comes in many forms. Success may be someone attending 15 meetings. That may be a very big success for that individual. Success may be defined as someone speaking in front of a group for the very first time. No matter how big or how small, true success is determined individually. During this meeting, we have an opportunity to share with others the successes we experienced as a result of our time together.

Administrative Duties and Details

If there are announcements, administrative details, voting, or distribution of materials, these duties are to be conducted before your meeting begins.

Peer Mentor Circles

(Read Aloud)

"PowerUp! and all GOGI studies are defined by our GOGI Calendar of Study and our Peer Mentor Circles. If we have not already done so, at this time we break from the larger group meeting into our Peer Mentor Circles of 5-12 participants."

Start Your Meeting

(Volunteer To Read Aloud)

"The GOGI Tools are studied worldwide according to the GOGI Calendar of Study. We unite with others according to this schedule, so no one will feel they are alone in their effort to make positive decisions. We believe in everyone's ability to benefit from this positive community of individuals united on the GOGI Calendar of Study. We call this Powerup! Tool Review Meeting to order."

The PowerUp! Purpose

(Volunteer To Read)

"The objective of PowerUp! Community Meetings is to reinforce the use of the GOGI Tools and support positive community experiences. We accomplish our objective through the study of the GOGI Tools shared in Peer Mentor Circles according to the GOGI Calendar of Study."

Peer Mentor Circle Review of the Tools

(Read In Peer Mentor Circles)

A volunteer recites or reads the GOGI Tools.

BOSS OF MY BRAIN
BELLY BREATHING
FIVE SECOND LIGHTSWITCH
POSITIVE THOUGHTS
POSITIVE WORDS
POSITIVE ACTIONS
CLAIM RESPONSIBILITY
LET GO
FOR-GIVE
WHAT IF
REALITY CHECK
ULTIMATE FREEDOM

In your Peer Mentor Circles, review the following questions and engage in discussions utilizing available GOGI materials or texts.

1) What are the names of the FOUR SETS OF TOOLS?

2) What Tools are in the set called TOOLS OF THE BODY?

3) What Tools are in the set called TOOLS OF CHOICE?

4) What Tools are in the set called TOOLS OF MOVING FORWARD?

5) What Tools are in the set called TOOLS OF CREATION?

6) What is your favorite Tool and why?

7) How many of the Tools can you name from memory?

8) Why do the Tools have KEY WORDS and can you recite any KEY WORDS for the Tools?

9) Why do GOGI studies rely on a calendar and what do you think about this?

10) Why were PowerUp! Community Meetings created?

11) Why is a PowerUp! Team Building Meeting held every fifteen meetings?

12) Why is a Tool Review Meeting held every fifteen meetings?

13) What might your Peer Mentor Circle want to do next week for the PowerUp! Success Celebration?

14) Recap in your own words the value you place on your PowerUp! Peer Mentor Circle experience.

The GOGI Pledge of Service (Read Aloud)

"All students of GOGI unite with our GOGI Pledge of Service. This pledge defines our purpose and is repeated at the end of every PowerUp! Community Meeting. Remaining in your Peer Mentor Circles, each group will rotate leading the pledge for the larger group. As we close this PowerUp! Community Meeting, we unite as a community with our pledge to be of service. Please repeat after me:"

May our commitment (repeat)
To the study of GOGI (repeat)
Grant us the joy (repeat)
Of giving and receiving (repeat)
So our inner freedom (repeat)
May be of maximum service (repeat)
To those we love (repeat)
And infinite others (repeat)

Tidy Up Time

(Read Aloud)

"We thank you for participating in this weeks PowerUp!. Our next meeting will be held (day/time/place) and since this was our Tool Recap Meeting, our next meeting we will Celebrate our Successes. Please let us leave this room clean and tidy for the next group."

PowerUp! Community Meeting
PowerUp!
Celebrate PowerUp! Successes
Hold this meeting: After The Tool Review

Administrative Duties and Details
If there are announcements, administrative details, voting, or distribution of materials, these tasks are to be conducted before your meeting begins.

Peer Mentor Circles
(Read Aloud)
"PowerUp! and all GOGI studies are defined by our GOGI Calendar of Study and our Peer Mentor Circles. If we have not already done so, at this time we break from the larger group meeting into our Peer Mentor Circles of 5-12 participants."

The PowerUp! Purpose
(Volunteer To Read)
"The objective of PowerUp! Community Meetings is to reinforce the use of the GOGI Tools and support positive community experiences. We accomplish our objective through the study of the GOGI Tools shared in Peer Mentor Circles according to the GOGI Calendar of Study."

Peer Mentor Circle Review of the Tools
(Read in Peer Mentor Circles)

A volunteer recites or reads the GOGI Tools.

BOSS OF MY BRAIN
BELLY BREATHING
FIVE SECOND LIGHTSWITCH
POSITIVE THOUGHTS
POSITIVE WORDS
POSITIVE ACTIONS
CLAIM RESPONSIBILITY
LET GO
FOR-GIVE
WHAT IF
REALITY CHECK
ULTIMATE FREEDOM

Celebrate
(To Be Read Aloud)

"To celebrate means to acknowledge progress, which is important when reinforcing lasting change. During this PowerUp! Celebrate Success, we acknowledge ourselves as individuals, as a Peer Mentor Circle, as a larger group, and as an entire community for the successes we have experienced in our previous 14 weeks together. If a formal outline has been developed for this meeting, we will now defer to that agenda. If not, we review the possible ways below to celebrate our individual and collective successes in our PowerUp!.

Activities

Possible activities to celebrate success are:

1. ### SHARE —
    Members share their favorite Tool and why.

2. ### RECITE —
    Each member recites as many Tools from memory as they can and a prize is offered to the individual with the most tools memorized.

3. ### DISCUSS —
    Members discuss Tools and cite examples of how they worked when applied.

4. ### ASK —
    Each member takes turn asking other members a question about a specific Tool.

5. ### ACKNOWLEDGE —
    One at a time, each member stands in the center of the circle and the other group members tells them what they have seen in that person's growth and improvement.

6. ### WRITE —
    The group writes thank you letters to the organization or institution or individual responsible for providing PowerUp! as an opportunity.

7. ### GOALS —
    The group permits each member to state their goals for the future.

8. ### OTHER —
    Make up your own way to acknowledge the progress of your group.

The GOGI Pledge of Service
(Read Aloud)

"All students of GOGI unite with our GOGI Pledge of Service. This pledge defines our purpose and is repeated at the end of every PowerUp! Community Meeting. Remaining in your Peer Mentor Circles, each group will rotate leading the pledge for the larger group.
As we close this PowerUp! Community Meeting, we unite as a community with our pledge to be of service. Please repeat after me:"

May our commitment (repeat)

To the study of GOGI (repeat)

Grant us the joy (repeat)

Of giving and receiving (repeat)

So our inner freedom (repeat)

May be of maximum service (repeat)

To those we love (repeat)

And infinite others (repeat)

Tidy Up Time
(Read Aloud)

"We thank you for participating in PowerUp!. Please let us leave this room clean and tidy for the next group. We acknowledge the completion of this round. Our next meeting will be the Team Building Meeting."

Letter to the PowerUp! Facilitator
From Coach Taylor, GOGI Founder

Dearest PowerUp! GOGI Certified Community Coach or PowerUp! Facilitator,

Thank you. Thank you for showing up as a solution in your community when it is so much easier to sit back and point the finger at problems. In stepping up as the solution, you are setting an excellent example that does not go unnoticed, even when you feel no one is looking.

Through your GOGI studies, you have learned to BE the solution and in doing so, you have come to realize that others will find the courage within themselves to PowerUp! as well. Congratulations. That, alone, makes a worthy and valuable life.

I sincerely hope you acknowledge yourself each night before you go to bed and are grateful that you have taken your journey this far, thanking, too, all the other aspects that are included in your successes, be it religion, culture, family, or a simple book which may have been read at just the right time in your life. Gratitude is like a magnet drawing more good things your way.

As you know, the student of GOGI understands the importance of gratitude, even for the smallest of life's graces. The student of GOGI sets aside blame, fault finding, and political positioning, as these often get in the way of a truly happy, meaningful, and purposeful life.

The GOGI student understands that when focused on all that is wrong, it is very difficult to see less noisy improvements that could be acted upon to make things better.

Indeed, the student of GOGI realizes a few fundamental facts:

1) Each of our lives on this precious little planet is very short, even though it seems endless in our youth;

2) Regardless of the limitations we feel, our lives can be filled with contentment through a shift in perspective that includes a realization of our enormous impact – for better or for worse - on the lives with which we come into contact;

3) Our GOGI Tools help us PowerUp! to our very best version of self so when our final day here on Earth has played itself out, we can complete our tenure truly realizing we lived a good and happy life.

In facilitating PowerUp!, you are making a stand for each human's innate potential for good, and their oftentimes buried hope that life can mean anything more than its current condition.

As a student of GOGI, you hold fast to seeing beyond the flaws and into the potential within each living human being to contribute positively to their environment. You do this with a clear focus of service, unwaveringly seeking even deeper ways you can positively impact the world in which you live.

Please, for a moment, catch the vision that has been burned into my mind as a reality in which I currently live. I have no challenge in seeing billions of human beings being taught that they are the masters of their bodies (TOOLS OF THE BODY), that they have the option to choose (TOOLS OF CHOICE), that they can move forward beyond any and all obstacles (TOOLS OF MOVING FORWARD) and that each and every human has a large amount of control over their life's outcome (TOOLS OF CREATION).

It is the GOGI Tools and their application I have watched transform lives since 2002. I became GOGI's first volunteer back then and realized the vision which has become the reality in which I live.

For me, these Tools, created from some of the darkest places on earth, have illuminated the simplicity of creating the optimal human existence. Know that I endeavor to utilize my GOGI Tools every minute of every day. Indeed, they have become a part of me and are impossible to set aside from my every breath.

Please realize, too, the culture of GOGI is unstoppable, and there will be similar and more initiatives like GOGI which enable the human to easily find great joy and purpose each day.

We humans ARE headed in a very positively powerful direction, even when it appears to be getting worse. Please know the roots of goodness are deep and powerful and will ultimately weather any storm. We are simply tested by adversity; we are not taken down by it.

Use your Tools daily. Let them become a part of your being, and never fail to PowerUp! in all you think, say and do. You ARE important. You ARE of great value. And, you ARE very much respected for your choices to step up as the solution, even at times when you feel no one is looking...

With Love,

Coach Taylor
GOGI's First Volunteer

About the Author
By Coach Taylor

Coach Taylor, GOGI Founder and GOGI's First Volunteer

To claim I am the author of this book is a necessary fact for identification purposes, but it is not the entire truth. The information in this book is not new, nor is it mine. The information in this book has been aggregated from hundreds of sources and collected through the contributions of thousands of individuals along their GOGI Journey toward internal freedom.

It may be more accurate to say I am the "aggregator" of existing information. As such, as the aggregator, it was suggested that more information be available about me, and how I became the GOGI aggregator.

The last thing I wanted to do was to answer questions about where I was born, or where I went to school. None of that matters much to me anymore, and I would hope such information would interest you even less.

What I want you to know about me is that I once suffered. Greatly. From my early childhood I saw pain and suffering that no one else around me seemed to notice. My family was brilliant at ignoring even the loudest cries for help. My schools were woefully inadequate at spotting the suffering child sitting in the back seat. My community was terribly preoccupied with superficial nonsense that seemed to be at the root of all their collective angst.

All this to say, I no longer suffer and I credit this reality to the daily use of my GOGI Tools. This author didn't so much "author" this book. This book may document my journey, but armed with my GOGI Tools I did, and will continue to, author my life. I invite you to do the same.